Curriculum Partner

Recent Titles in
Greenwood Professional Guides in School Librarianship

How to Teach about American Indians: A Guide for the School Library Media Specialist
Karen D. Harvey with Lisa D. Harjo and Lynda Welborn

100 Research Topic Guides for Students
Barbara Wood Borne

Special Events Programs in School Library Media Centers: A Guide to Making Them Work
Marcia Trotta

Information Services for Secondary Schools
Dana McDougald and Melvin Bowie

The Internet and the School Library Media Specialist: Transforming Traditional Services
Randall M. MacDonald

Creating a Local Area Network in the School Library Media Center
Becky R. Mather

Collection Assessment and Management for School Libraries: Preparing for Cooperative Collection Development
Debra E. Kachel

Using Educational Technology with At-Risk Students: A Guide for Library Media Specialists and Teachers
Roxanne Baxter Mendrinos

Teaching Electronic Literacy: A Concepts-Based Approach for School Library Media Specialists
Kathleen W. Craver

Block Scheduling and Its Impact on the School Library Media Center
Marie Keen Shaw

Using Internet Primary Sources to Teach Critical Thinking Skills in History
Kathleen W. Craver

100 More Research Topic Guides for Students
Dana McDougald

Curriculum Partner
Redefining the Role of the Library Media Specialist

Carol A. Kearney

Greenwood Professional Guides in School Librarianship
Harriet Selverstone, Series Adviser

GREENWOOD PRESS
Westport, Connecticut • London

Library of Congress Cataloging-in-Publication Data

Kearney, Carol A., 1939–
  Curriculum partner : redefining the role of the library media specialist / by Carol A. Kearney.
      p.   cm.—(Greenwood professional guides in school librarianship, ISSN 1074–150X)
    Includes bibliographical references (p.) and index.
    ISBN 0–313–31025–4 (alk. paper)
    1. School libraries—United States.   2. Curriculum planning—United States.   3. Instructional materials centers—United States.   4. Teacher-librarians—United States.
    I. Title.   II. Series.
  Z675.S3   K42   2000
  027.8—dc21   99–462341

British Library Cataloguing in Publication Data is available.

Library of Congress Catalog Card Number: 99–462341
ISBN: 0–313–31025–4
ISSN: 1074–150X

First published in 2000

Greenwood Press, 88 Post Road West, Westport, CT 06881
An imprint of Greenwood Publishing Group, Inc.
www.greenwood.com

Printed in the United States of America

The paper used in this book complies with the
Permanent Paper Standard issued by the National
Information Standards Organization (Z39.48–1984).

10 9 8 7 6 5 4 3 2 1

This book is dedicated to my Mom, Inez Lenore Schubring, who has been my role model in everything I do; whose loving encouragement and support gave me the knowledge that I could do whatever I set my mind to do, and the courage to follow through; whose spiritual understanding, perseverance, sincerity, and integrity have been used as a yardstick against which to measure my life.

I also wish to dedicate this book to my husband, Jack, for his loving patience during this year; to our children, Yvonne Pingitore and Jack Kearney III, and their spouses, Joe and Anne, respectively; and to our grandchildren: Jaclyn, Jordan, and John Pingitore, all of whom are the light of my life.

Contents

Preface

Students who are in elementary schools today will ultimately work at jobs that have not been defined as yet. Although classroom teachers and library media specialists will be unable to prepare students, at this time, by providing specific training, they can prepare them to "learn how to learn" by becoming information literate—to access, evaluate, and use information effectively; to be able to cope with change; and to identify and derive solutions to problems. The library media specialist, who is a curriculum partner and an integral member of the instructional team, is a catalyst in this process, which is founded in the mission of the library media program.

The mission of the library media program is to ensure that students and staff are effective users of ideas and information. This mission is accomplished:

• by providing intellectual and physical access to materials in all formats

• by providing instruction to foster competence and stimulate interest in reading, viewing, and using information and ideas

• by working with other educators to design learning strategies to meet the needs of individual students. (AASL & AECT, 1988, 1)

Although it was developed in 1988, this remains the mission statement of our profession today. It is found in *Information Power: Building Partnerships for Learning* (1998, 6), published by the American Association of School Librarians (AASL) and the Association for Educational Communications and Technology (AECT).

If we are to prepare students to function in the 21st century and to ensure that students as well as staff fulfill the mission of the media program, we must overcome the barriers that would keep us from our goal. *Information Power: Guidelines for School Library Media Programs* (AASL & AECT, 1988) defined three roles of the library media specialist: teacher, information specialist, and instructional consultant. Whereas the first two roles included traditional responsibilities of library media specialists, many found the instructional consultant role more challenging. Even those who had been cooperatively planning curricular projects with teachers found it difficult to implement. Many library media specialists read the literature, attended library media conferences, and attempted to incorporate much of what they learned within their programs. They regarded the library media center as an extension of the classroom; planned subject-area as well as interdisciplinary projects with teachers and integrated library and information skills into the context of the content; worked to meet teachers and students at their point of need; felt they were members of the instructional team; experienced support from the principal; and were members of schoolwide committees. Yet research demonstrates that the role of instructional consultant was only minimally accepted by teachers, administrators, and library media specialists themselves.

CURRENT STATE OF THE LIBRARY MEDIA CENTER

According to research conducted during the 1990s, this situation continues to prevail. Few school principals feel that the library media specialist has much influence over curriculum decisions (Ingersoll & Han, 1994, 36); with few exceptions, principals think that library media specialists are not involved in instructional planning at a consistent level (Wolcott, 1994, 161). Although library media specialists believe they regularly function as information specialist and teacher, they see the role of instructional consultant as a more informal part of their role (DeGroff, 1997, 18). When elementary library media specialists are used to provide planning time for teachers, those specialists spend significantly less time in consultation and in teaching information skills than when their schedules are flexible (Tallman & Donham van Deusen, 1994b, 31).

Furthermore, the literature indicates that most teachers and administrators have a very limited understanding of the library media center and how it functions. Gary N. Hartzell (1994) suggests that teachers perceive the library media center as a program that responds to the needs of others. They do not see it as a vehicle for defining their subject area needs (11). He continues, "teachers and administrators do not consciously deny you the opportunity to function as teacher, staff developer, or instructional consultant. It is simply they don't think of you in those

terms" (11). In addition, few teacher or administrator preparation programs address the importance of the library media program or the role
of the library media specialist in curriculum, instruction, staff development, or administrative support. Hartzell concludes that library media
programs and specialists are thought of as "adjuncts rather than as integrated components of quality teaching and learning experiences, they
are not visibly identified with the central core of school activities" (12).

Before library media specialists were able to implement this role, and
before teachers and administrators had a chance to accept it, another
wave of change swept over us—technology, the Internet, and all its attendant advantages. Technology and telecommunications are presently
impacting many aspects of our lives. Even though the use of technology
in education is in its infancy, it is developing rapidly. Already it is a
vehicle in the restructuring of the educational program, helping us to
deliver the instructional program more efficiently and effectively. Technology is helping to actively involve students in their learning, thereby
utilizing problem solving and critical thinking skills that will help them
become information literate and lifelong learners. The Internet and the
World Wide Web are changing the way teachers teach and library media
specialists deliver programs.

In 1998, *Information Power: Building Partnerships for Learning* was presented to the library media community, further delineating our role
while identifying "Information Literacy Standards for Student Learning."
Our role—as teacher, instructional partner, information specialist, and
program administrator—continues to expand. Even though many library
media specialists are successfully functioning in this role, are seeing
changed perceptions among teachers and administrators, and are using
technology as a learning tool, there is a serious need to provide a resource that will assist others to fully function in this role.

HOW WILL THIS BOOK HELP ME FUNCTION AS
A LIBRARY MEDIA SPECIALIST IN THE 21st CENTURY?

As library media specialists, we all have had visions of "the way it
could be": demonstrating our leadership regularly; creating a partnership with both the principal and other administrators so that support for
the program is present; understanding the change process and using it
to be an agent of change; developing a broad base of support for our
program by creating vision, mission, goals, and objectives in collaboration with members of our learning community; collaborating and functioning as a full partner with classroom teachers in the planning,
implementation, and assessment of the instructional program; establishing our expertise in areas such as technology by providing staff development for colleagues and others; and building a local as well as a

far-reaching advocacy network. This book provides the reader with the tools to achieve this vision. *Curriculum Partner: Redefining the Role of the Library Media Specialist* presents supportive research, theory, and concepts; offers practical examples gathered from interviews with library media specialists on the forefront of redefining this changing role; and concludes with strategies for implementing this role.

Chapter 1   The Library Media Specialist: Redefining Leadership

Key to working as a curriculum partner is the ability to lead. Empowerment, power bases, influence, and organizational politics are important forces that are described.

Chapter 2   A Partnership with the Principal: Redefining Support for the Library Media Program

It is critical to both create a partnership with the principal and have his or her support in the development and implementation of the library media program. An action plan, designed to engage the support of the principal in strengthening the library media program, is outlined.

Chapter 3   The Change Process: Redefining the Library Media Program

The chapter begins with a survey of current research and literature on change, continues by providing two school library media models, and concludes with information on locally based research.

Chapter 4   Vision, Mission, Goals, and Objectives: Redefining Planning

The first step in the development of any program involves (1) the creation of a vision consistent with the mission of the organization, and (2) the formulation of long- and short-term program goals and objectives. These working tools must be conceived by library media specialists in collaboration with members of their learning community.

Chapter 5   Collaborative Planning: Redefining a Partnership with Teachers

The planning process (the first step in instructional design), as well as the tools necessary to be a curriculum partner in the planning process, are detailed in this chapter. The role of curriculum, collaborative planning, resource-based learning, and information literacy standards—all important steps in the process—are examined.

Chapter 6   Program Implementation and Assessment: Redefining the Instructional Program

The last steps in instructional design—program implementation and assessment—are explained. Research processes, use of technology as a learning tool, interdisciplinary curriculum, cooperative learning, learning styles, and alternative assessment models are discussed.

Chapter 7   Staff Development: Redefining Opportunities for Learning

The dual role of the library media specialist as student and teacher of continuing educational opportunities is explored. Collaboration, leadership, and partnering are critical elements of a successful staff development program.

Chapter 8   Advocacy: Redefining a Community of Supporters

Building an advocacy network within the school and its community, as well as within the political and professional communities, will broaden the scope of the program, make it more dynamic, and guarantee its continuing support as well as growth.

Acknowledgments

During my adventure of this past year, many friends and colleagues were instrumental in bringing this book to fruition. I wish to acknowledge their assistance. Ann Fronckowiak, Carol Kroll, and Carole Sedita shared their wisdom and provided extraordinary feedback, insight, and advice as they read chapters of the book. I am deeply grateful for their contributions.

There were many people who supplied resources, information, and recommendations—Carolyn Giambra; Cathy Hetzler; David Loertscher; Geri Mycio; Carol Pace; Sandy Pezzino; Patricia Webster; Blanche Woolls; the librarians at the Orchard Park Public Library, Orchard Park, New York; the Interlibrary Loan Department of the Buffalo and Erie County Public Library, Buffalo, New York; the Largo Public Library, in Largo, Florida; and many, many more who have shared their ideas, support, and love. I have been able to complete the adventure because of their assistance.

I am indebted to the library media practitioners who are working on the cutting edge of our profession and who have shared their experiences throughout this book. Their stories make the theory come alive.

Last, I want to recognize the work of Debra Adams, Acquisitions Editor, Greenwood Publishing Group, Inc., and Harriet Selverstone, series advisor for the Greenwood Professional Guides in School Librarianship, for their guidance throughout the year. I am sincerely appreciative of their patience, excellent counsel, and continual encouragement.

Introduction: A Time of Change

There was a time when graduates accepted jobs immediately after college and remained in that position for their entire career with the job description varying only slightly during that time. Today, projections indicate that people entering the work force will change their job titles four or five times during their career. The skills required of these people are very different from those required of their predecessors. Change is occurring at a rapid rate and will escalate in the years to come.

The changes library media specialists have experienced during the past forty years are remarkable, transforming their roles from librarian to library media specialist and their programs in myriad ways—from a book depository in the 1960s; to a library media center with audiovisual materials, the emerging philosophy of service to teachers, and the support of the intructional programs in the 1970s; to the integration of information skills into the context of the instructional program, resource-based learning, and the incorporation of curriculum development in the job description for the library media specialist in the 1980s; to the instructional consulting and partner role and the integration of numerous types of technology in the 1990s. Most library media specialists have retrained themselves and reorganized their positions several times during their careers. Few other professionals can attest to such development while remaining in the same position. This metamorphosis is truly exceptional and will continue.

EDUCATORS AND RESEARCHERS OF THE 1990S

The changes that library media specialists have experienced were in direct response to research and practice embedded in educational reform during these forty years. Educators and researchers have made significant strides during the 1990s toward reform as well. Following is a selective list of experts and/or research that have guided educational reform and that will guide the library media profession during the 21st century.

Michael G. Fullan

Michael G. Fullan (1991) details research that documents the change process: what it is, how to plan for it, how to cope with it, and how to make it happen. This compendium of research is vital to educators and library media specialists as they initiate change.

Peter M. Senge

Peter M. Senge (1990) describes how "learning organizations" can be built by subscribing to five components or disciplines: (1) systems thinking, which addresses the conceptual framework or the whole rather than any part of the pattern; (2) personal mastery, whereby people and organizations are committed to "lifelong learning," continually clarifying things that matter to them and then living according to their highest goals; (3) approaches whereby people continually challenge, evaluate, and scrutinize their models and then share them with others; (4) building shared vision among the school community, which fosters genuine commitment rather than simple compliance; and (5) team learning, which begins with "dialogue" among team members and in which the combined intelligences of the team are greater than that of its members. The team is the fundamental learning unit in the modern organization (6–10). Senge's "learning organizations" are central to educational reform as well as to the integration of the library media program within the instructional program.

The Constructivist Movement

The Constructivist movement of the late 1980s and early 1990s places the student in the center of the learning process and environment and considers how students learn, how teachers teach, and how understandings are constructed. These theories are discussed in *In Search of Understanding: The Case for Constructivist Classrooms* (Brooks & Brooks, 1993, 3–4). The authors present five principles: (1) posing problems that are relevant to students; (2) organizing learning around broad ideas or concepts; (3) requesting and valuing students' ideas and assumptions; (4) modifying curriculum to address these assumptions; and (5) assessing student learning as part of the teaching process (viii). According to Constructivists, students' construction of new understandings from prior knowledge is the underpinning of education. An integrated, curriculum-based library media program can be easily developed in collaboration with teachers by utilizing the Constructivists' philosophy.

LIBRARY RESEARCH AND MODELS

Research has been conducted and paradigms proposed by leaders in the library media and reading fields which will continue to guide the creation of quality library media programming in the 21st century.

Resource-Based Learning

In 1982 the Ministry of Education in Ontario, Canada, published a document entitled *Partners in Action: The Library Resource Centre in the School Curriculum*. It described resource-based learning as a process that engages students in meaningful learning activities that have been planned by the classroom teacher and library media specialist utilizing a broad range of appropriate print, nonprint, and human resources to provide a curriculum selected by professionals in the school. Resource-based learning addresses the diversity of student abilities and interests by providing for individual differences and styles of learning. The approach recognizes that students are active learners in their instructional program, gaining satisfaction from their accomplishments as well as self-confidence and independence (*Partners in Action*, 1982, 6–9). This concept has become the program of choice in many library media programs nationally and internationally.

David Loertscher

David Loertscher (1988) presented taxonomies of the school library media program that divided qualitative services into eleven steps or levels. Levels 1 and 2 form the warehouse block. Levels 3 to 7 focus on direct service to teachers and students. Levels 8 to 11 are the building blocks of resource-based teaching (11).

Loertscher regards the last four levels as integral to an effective library media program. In level 8 (scheduled planning) the library media specialist is involved in planning with the classroom teacher for the purpose of supplying resources for a previously planned unit. In level 9 (instructional design, level I) the library media specialist participates in each step of the creation, implementation, and assessment of the instructional unit. The library media center is considered enrichment. In level 10 (instructional design, level II) the library media specialist participates in the creation of resource-based units in which the complete unit content is dependent on the resources and activities of the library media program. In level 11 (curriculum development, the highest level of the taxonomy) the library media specialist is recognized as a leader and is a principal contributor to the instructional program of the school (1988, 13). It is incumbent on the library media specialist to move individual teachers up through the taxonomy to create a more responsive library media program.

Ken Haycock

Ken Haycock (1992) has compiled doctoral research associated with instructional effectiveness of the library media specialist or teacher-librarian and library media center in a publication entitled *What Works: Research About Teaching and Learning Through the School's Library Resource Center*. The book presents the results of research in a format that is easy to read as well as easy to share with colleagues and decisionmakers in school districts. The book is modeled after a publication with the same name by the U.S. Department of Education (*What Works*, 1986). For each topic there are research findings, comments, and references. Haycock's valuable publication makes research accessible to library media specialists and library media committees as they create new or change existing library media programs.

Philip Turner

Philip Turner (1993) defines four levels of interaction with teachers in instructional consultation. At No Involvement the teacher asks the library media specialist for no assistance, or, the library media specialist is unable or unwilling to provide assistance. At the Initial Level there is little or no interaction between the classroom teacher and the library media specialist. The library media specialist develops and maintains the collection, equipment, and facility. At the Moderate Level there are some interactions with the classroom teacher, but they are short in duration and include only some of the steps in instructional design. At the In-Depth Level there are extensive interactions with the classroom teacher in which the library media specialist may serve as a team member in the instructional program and is involved in all steps of instructional design (17). Like Loertscher, Turner provides information about programming that will help the library media specialist achieve one of these levels with each classroom teacher and then move that teacher up to the next level, continually improving the library media program for students and teachers.

Keith Curry Lance,
Lynda Welborn, and Christine Hamilton-Pennell

A group of researchers from the Colorado Public Schools—Keith Curry Lance, Lynda Welborn, and Christine Hamilton-Pennell (1992)—presented findings of a study that provides evidence of the positive influence of library media centers (LMCs) on academic achievement in 221 Colorado public schools during the 1988–1989 school year (iii). In examining the influence of school library media centers on academic achievement, the authors report the following:

- The size of a library media center's staff and collection is the best school predictor of academic achievement.
- The instructional role of the library media specialist shapes the collection and, in turn, academic achievement.
- The degree of collaboration between library media specialist and teachers is affected by the ratio of teachers to pupils.
- Library media expenditures affect LMC staff and collection size and, in turn, academic achievement.
- Library media expenditures and staffing vary with total school expenditures and staffing.
- Among school and community predictors of academic achievement, the size of the LMC staff and collection is second only to the absence of at-risk conditions, particularly poverty and low educational attainment among adults (Lance, Welborn, & Hamilton-Pennell, 1992, 96).

In addition, these researchers' work in 1997 indicates that students in schools with well-staffed library media programs, including library media specialists supported with library aides and playing a vital instructional role by complementing the work of classroom teachers, averaged reading scores 5 to 10 points higher than those without such staffing (Fast Facts, 1998, 1, 2).

Stephen Krashen

Research conducted by Stephen Krashen (1993) found that free voluntary reading is the foundation of language education. In studies in which students engaged in free voluntary reading—that is, sustained silent reading and self-directed reading—readers did better in reading comprehension, writing style, vocabulary, spelling, and grammatical development. Furthermore, having access to a school library media center and a school library media specialist resulted in more reading by the students. The larger the school library media collection from which students selected books to read, the higher the reading scores of those students (12, 34, 38).

CONCLUSION

The research findings, theories, and practice summarized here are the building blocks of the philosophy, concepts, and strategies presented in this book. Together they can be used to derive an exemplary library media program. Such a program will facilitate educational reform in the schools. Library media specialists and library media committees across the country can use *Curriculum Partner: Redefining the Role of the Library Media Specialist* when developing library media programs for the 21st century.

The Library Media Specialist: Redefining Leadership

1

During the last forty years, our society has moved from an industrial to a technological, information-based society. Skills needed to function in this age have changed dramatically, but the ultimate goal of education is still the same: to ensure that students are literate adults when they graduate from high school. To achieve this goal in a technological age, students must become information literate: able to access, evaluate, and use information (AASL & AECT, 1998, 1).

To ensure that students become information literate, the library media center must be an integral component of students' learning and assessment; the library media specialist must be a full curriculum partner with classroom teachers in this process; information literacy standards must be integrated into all curricular areas; students must be at the center of their instructional program; and technology must be used effectively to facilitate student learning. For this vision to become a reality, the library media specialist must step forward and accept the challenge to become a leader and/or to exercise leadership skills consistently.

WHAT IS LEADERSHIP?

Although historians, social scientists, biographers, and educational researchers have studied the concept of leadership for decades, consensus is still lacking on exactly what it is and how it should be analyzed (Gibson, Ivancevich, & Donnelly, 1988, 371). For the purpose of discussion in this book, leadership is the process whereby an individual has an idea, a goal, or a vision and shares it with others, who make the vision their own and draw others to it while the original leader finds ways to celebrate their success.

To become a full member of the teaching team—that is, a curriculum partner—the library media specialist must learn to become a leader—to integrate leadership skills into his or her repertoire of professional and personal skills. Although the literature identifies many characteristics, those that follow are highly important.

Inspiring a Vision

Leadership begins when an individual has a vision or dream of "the way it could be" and can inspire others to share this vision or dream. The leader is able to develop the vision because he or she is continually reading, learning, and reflecting on new ideas. Before sharing the vision with others the leader reviews the literature, considers both the positive and negative aspects of it, identifies the benefits, and consults with people who have successfully implemented programs based on it. Reflection and analysis are pivotal to the success of the vision.

When the leader shares this vision with others, they interpret it in relationship to their own goals and roles that are meaningful to them (Blanchard, Carlos, & Randolph, 1996, 56). As these people understand and agree with the vision, they make it their own when they see where their contributions make a difference (49). As they share the vision with others, they feel empowered because they understand and accept it as their own. As they draw other people to their vision, these others respond in terms of their own goals and roles, and the process continues (56). Ultimately the people who are inspired by the vision become its "cheerleaders," and together they "invent the future" (Kouzes & Posner, 1987, 9). The leader finds ways of celebrating their accomplishments.

Understanding and accepting the vision, which are primary to its integration, are empowering. The key is to empower everyone in the organization with information so they will respond intelligently to a new idea or vision when it is presented.

Sharon Vansickle is a library media specialist and technology coordinator at Norcross High School (a school of 2,200 students) in the Gwinnett County School District, a suburban district in Lawrenceville, Georgia. Sharon describes the leadership of the three library media specialists:

The library media staff at Norcross is working to create partnerships with our teachers through collaborative planning, implementation, and assessment of instructional programs. Many teachers are using both resource-based teaching and resource-based learning. Teachers use a wide range of resources to teach their subject matter (resource-based teaching) as well as involve students in their own learning by providing activities collaboratively planned with the library media staff, to bring the students and resources together through an instructional unit (resource-based learning). The unit or project culminates in a product, which is then shared with the class. Students often use technology for this presentation.

Our goal is to move teachers toward an independent level of technology use as well as for them to assume some leadership in this area within their department [vision]. Once a teacher has received staff development from one of our staff, although we are still willing to work with them again, we are hopeful that they will, in turn, work with other colleagues so that we, the library media staff, may branch out and involve even more teachers in the collaborative process [sharing the vision]. The best example of this happening is in our social studies department. We have teachers who are actively involved in integrating technology into their curriculum [making the vision their own]. Depending on the unit they are studying, students produce presentations which they give to the class using PowerPoint and Free Lance Graphics; or they create publications using a desktop publishing program. Students use resources to find information and put together assessment pieces that really do demonstrate what they are learning.

What has happened over the past five years is that as we have worked with these teachers, the projects have gotten better and better. Because of their work with technology and the recognition of their expertise by other teachers, they have begun to work more cooperatively with colleagues in their department and have either involved these people in projects or referred them to us so we can begin the collaborative process with new teachers [drawing others to their vision]. Our library media staff has looked for ways to recognize and reward these wonderful people through certificates and our annual M.U.T.T. Award (Making Use of Technology in Teaching) [celebrating their accomplishments]. The numbers who collaboratively plan continue to grow. We are grateful to see "our vision" become "their vision." (Sharon Vansickle, personal communication, May 10, 1999)

Using Good Communication and Group Process Skills

In order to share the vision with others, the leader must have the ability to communicate it effectively. Being able to employ the skills of good communication honestly and with no effort, at the moment they are needed, is an empowering goal. In a profession based on information, we may be engaged in oral communication for more than three-quarters of our time, questioning and giving information (Herrin, Pointon, & Russell, 1986, 80, 81). Therefore we must become expert in interpersonal communications. To be a good communicator we must understand our individual communication style (e.g., intuitor, thinker, feeler, or sensor); develop the skills of active listening by both listening and responding in a way that lets the other person (i.e., the sender) know that nothing else is important at that moment other than listening to him or her; using paraphrasing to help both the sender and receiver of a message clarify its meaning; providing feedback by describing our own reactions to another's message rather than being judgmental of the sender; and demonstrating empathy so that others feel we understand and are sympathetic to their position (Mycio, 1994a, 1–24; Mycio, 1994b, 1–25).

The leader also is one who both understands and is able to facilitate group process skills or decisionmaking skills. The ability to facilitate these processes derives from a mastery of communication skills. Group process skills including consensus building, problem solving, and conflict resolution enable people to review many options, evaluate them in light of criteria germane to a particular problem, select those options that will best facilitate achievement of the goal, and manage conflict during the process. Formal training is needed if skills are lacking in any of these areas. Good communication and group process skills take time to develop and integrate. However, they are paramount to the ability to function successfully and effectively as a leader.

Demonstrating Trust

In addition to having a vision and being able to communicate it effectively, the leader must consistently demonstrate trust in order to draw people to the vision. Trust develops gradually over time through honest interactions with people. If we earn the trust of others by demonstrating honesty, constancy, self-respect, and integrity, they will in turn trust us and feel that we are open, credible, and caring. When we present a new idea, they will be more inclined to support it because of the trust established between us. Once we have developed this type of relationship, we will be better able to communicate and work together (Covey, 1992, 31).

Being Competent and Continually Learning

The leader demonstrates competence and expertise when working with others; in fact, they are drawn to the leader because of this competence. As leaders we must demonstrate determination and perseverance in completing any task. To remain competent we must be continually learning—reading, attending seminars, and talking with colleagues, constantly expanding our competence, skills, abilities, and interests to ensure that others will recognize us as a leader (Covey, 1992, 33; Senge, 1990, 4). If we have already demonstrated competence in some area, when we share a new idea, goal, or vision people will listen because of our previously demonstrated competence.

Developing Effective Personal Skills

Leaders must develop effective personal skills as well. A leader treats everyone fairly. Friendship and personal prejudice do not affect the way we deal with others. Being fair means that we are consistent (Curzon, 1989, 33). We work to maintain a friendship with everyone, and we remove ourselves from cliques. We know our school's faculty and administration so that we are able to provide service at their point of need. We work to resolve problems constructively while making everyone feel welcome and comfortable in our presence. We have a sense of humor. Because we are unceasingly positive, people are drawn to and energized by our optimistic attitude and perspective—by our passion about what we do. We have high self-esteem, are confident in our ability, and regard ourselves as acceptable to others. Becoming aware of our strengths and talents that help us perform more effectively as persons and in our jobs will improve our self-esteem (Martin, 1982, 53).

A leader also respects the expertise of others and recognizes their contributions, finding ways for them to share in the rewards and celebrate the accomplishments. Rosabeth Moss Kanter (1987) describes this as sharing credit and recognition with all participants and "making everyone a hero."

In a study conducted in 1986, researchers identified characteristics of model library media specialists. The composite of the successful library media specialist is one who:

- Has a positive self-concept
- May be shy/reserved but projects warmth
- Is bright, stable, enthusiastic, experimenting/exploring, trusting
- Is able to be self-sufficient
- Is confident of worth as an individual
- Enjoys people, work, variety/diversity
- Views change as a positive challenge
- Values communication
- Communicates effectively as an individual
- Is caring and especially attentive to others
- Is able and willing to clarify communication
- Is relatively self-disclosing
- Is uncomfortable with conflict
- Is confident of ability to deal with difficult situations in professional manner
- Is neither critical nor domineering

• Has no great need for achievement, power, or economic advantage
• Views self as leader in curriculum development
• Is willing to take the risks of being a leader (Herrin et al., 1986, 86–87)

Although these characteristics cannot be generalized to all library media specialists, it is important to strive toward the positive image they project.

Donna L. Peterson, director of library media services for the Lincoln Public Schools, in Lincoln, Nebraska, which was a participant in the De-witt Wallace—Reader's Digest Fund National Library Power initiative (a 10-year, $40 million investment to revitalize school library media centers across the country), concludes from her many and varied experiences that

the most important element that determines success in library media programs is the individual skill and flexible, welcoming personality of the library media specialist. The most successful library media specialists are those who can appreciate and are able to work with all the personality types in an organization; those who are empathetic toward others and, as a result, can provide services that best meet the various expectations. They are also people who care deeply about students and their success. (Donna L. Peterson, personal communication, February 8, 1999)

Harlene Rosenberg, supervisor, Instructional Media Center, Hunter-don Central Regional High School (grades 9–12), Flemington, New Jersey, attributes the success of collaboration with teachers in her school on "a very friendly and outgoing group of library media specialists. We are honest, open, and respect the needs of the students and staff." Although she admits that they are not subject-area experts, they are "the in-house experts in the development and teaching of information skills and collection development" (Harlene Rosenberg, personal communication, January 8, 1999). These library media specialists have successfully assimilated and are demonstrating many leadership characteristics. Others in the building have recognized their competence.

CAN ANYONE OTHER THAN ADMINISTRATORS BE LEADERS?

School reform has affected many areas of school organization and program. One outcome is that teachers have emerged as leaders. Some teacher leaders are library media specialists. As organizations become less hierarchical and people feel empowered by the information that has been shared with them, everyone can be a teacher leader—and this leadership will flow throughout the organization depending on the circumstance. Those in the "middle" are already leading and will more frequently step forward and take the initiative. According to Ackerman (1996), teacher leadership has developed from three sources. First, teachers have utilized new methods of teaching that are based on research, thereby gaining greater credibility among their peers. Cooperative learning is an example of a new method of teaching. As teachers developed confidence in cooperative learning, they shared these ideas with other teachers, who in turn came into the teacher leaders' classrooms to observe the process and left with new ideas that they could put into practice (1, 2).

Second, teacher leadership has evolved because of the pervasive use of site-based decisionmaking for school improvement. Although the teams are representative of the entire learning community—administrators, teachers, parents, and community leaders—it is the teachers who most often implement the suggested plans. As teachers recognize their influence, they emerge as leaders of the process. Many library media specialists who are members of site-based teams, as well as chairs of their team, function as informal leaders and influence the work of school improvement (Ackerman, 1996, 2).

Rebecca Jones, a teacher leader and library media specialist at Gridley Middle School, a participant in the Library Power initiative (with approximately 800 students) in the Tucson Unified School District, a large urban school district in Tucson, Arizona, explains:

I view leadership as key to a successful library media program. Because I am the only library media specialist in my school, I want members of the learning community to see me in a variety of roles that help the school. I have been an active member of the site-based leadership team in my school from its inception and served as chair of the team for two years. This experience has helped the school community view me as a person who looks beyond the media center needs to the needs of the school as a whole. It also gives me a wider perspective. Librarians, as "onlys," can become quite isolated unless they reach out in a variety of ways. (Rebecca Jones, personal communication, January 2, 1999)

Third, teacher leadership has emerged as a result of the involvement of teachers in networks or consortia of similar-type schools. For example, the Coalition of Essential Schools promotes teacher leadership through a variety of activities. As teachers begin to share with others outside their schools, they recognize how much assistance they have to offer one another. They begin to take responsibility for the accomplishment of projects rather than relying on the administrator to be the single contributor of leadership within a building. As they share with teachers from other schools, they learn that there are many others who are committed to the same goals (Ackerman, 1996, 2).

Teacher leaders have also assumed leadership roles in departments and grade levels at the building level as well as in district-level projects. The library media specialist may be one of these teacher leaders who is a member or chair of a site-based decisionmaking or leadership team; or engages other teachers in collaborative planning that results in better curriculum projects or authentic learning experiences; or builds skill and confidence in others by discussing and sharing visions.

Leadership in the future will not rely exclusively on the principal at the school level or on the superintendent at the district level; rather, it will emerge from all levels and people. Teacher leaders, library media leaders, are already sharing the responsibility. People in the "middle" will help to implement school reform, and as a result students will better attain their instructional goals.

LEADING FROM THE MIDDLE: I AM NOT IN CHARGE. CAN I REALLY INFLUENCE MY SITUATION?

Geoffrey Bellman, a corporate consultant and author of a book entitled *Getting Things Done When You Are Not in Charge* (1992), assures us that people in the middle can get things done, can be leaders. Influence is one of the qualities that leaders in the middle use to persuade others to adopt a particular point of view and to bring about change.

To develop the quality of influence, you must begin by believing that what you do is a critical element in the instructional program; that without your work, teachers and students cannot achieve their goals; that you positively impact the lives of others; that you are competent and effective; that you are happy and satisfied in your job as well as committed to it; that you can influence your situation as well as your surroundings; and that your job is a positive part of your life. If you do not feel this way about your job and its relationship to the instructional program, this will be evident to the people around you: administrators, teachers, students, and parents—the learning community. Furthermore, you need to do something about it: talk to a mentor; take college classes, seminars, and professional development programs; and visit library media specialists to discuss elements of their success. If after this effort you still feel the same lack of passion and commitment, perhaps you need to seek another profession. Without passion and commitment to and belief in the value of your job as well as the contribution you make to students and the instructional program, you will not be able to lead others into the library media program that students need to function in the 21st century.

You work in an organization where you share the challenge of teaching students both the academic knowledge and the social skills needed to become successful lifelong learning adults. You have special skills and tools to help both teacher and student in the accomplishment of their instructional goals. You must influence both groups to make full use of the opportunities found in the media center. "By fostering information literacy and authentic learning among students and others," you encourage "members of the learning community to acquire knowledge and skills that will enhance their own contributions to school and society" (AASL & AECT, 1998, 53).

Even though you are in the middle in the school hierarchy, you should note that the principal is in the middle of the district hierarchy. You could say that you are not in charge and therefore have no power or influence. If the principal said this, the school would be in chaos. However, this is not true for either the principal or yourself. There is, in fact, something you can do. You must be actively engaged in implementing the following suggestions.

Develop Your Power Bases

Leaders are people whom others follow. One reason for this is that the leader uses power bases, which are potential means of successfully influencing the behavior of others (Mycio, 1992, 20). In order to lead from the middle, you must develop your power bases. The power bases described here are those from which library media specialists most often work. You may work from each of them under different circumstances and in different combinations. It is important to understand their potential for influencing others and to use them effectively.

Information power is based on your access to information that others consider valuable. If the library media collection has been developed collaboratively with teachers and in response to curricular needs, teachers and students will seek you out and ask for assistance in accessing and managing information. This is the power base from which you work during the majority of your day (Mycio, 1992, 20).

Expert power is based on a special skill, knowledge, or expertise that you demonstrate and that is highly regarded and sought after. Experts have power even if they have a low status in the hierarchy. The more difficult it is to replace the expert, the greater the amount of power the expert possesses. If you are an expert in technology, for example, you will have a great amount of expert power and people will search you out (Gibson, Ivancevich, & Donnelly, 1988, 336).

Referent power is based on personal traits. Charisma is the basis of referent power. The strength of your charisma is an indicator of how much referent power you have. If you have developed these personal traits, you will have another power base from which to work and influence others (Gibson, Ivancevich, & Donnelly, 1988, 336).

Connection power is based on the association you may have to an influential person either within or outside the organization. This relationship may provide you with an additional power base from which to work (Mycio, 1992, 20).

Determine on Whom You Are Dependent

One of the characteristics of the position of library media specialist is that your accomplishment is dependent on the accomplishment of others. You are in the business of helping teachers and students be successful. Of course, you expect to succeed as well. However, this is not a given. When leading from the middle, you need to step back from your situation and determine exactly on whom you are dependent for success— and then develop a plan of action to gain his or her support (Hartzell, 1994, 3, 4). Even if you develop the greatest collection housed in the most attractive facility and organized for easy access, if no one uses it, it is worthless. In times of plenty, funding will continue to flow to the library media center. However, in times of financial need, the leaders in the school and school district will stop the flow of funds and may even eliminate the professional position. You cannot wait for teachers to recognize the importance of the library media program to their success; you need to take the initiative and begin to build your influence.

Gary Hartzell, in his book entitled *Building Influence for the School Librarian* (1994), has detailed the process by which to identify the "network of power and influence" that affects the library media specialist. He suggests drawing a diagram of the people and positions on whom success as a library media specialist depends, determine the relationship to them, and initiate a campaign to influence them. Hartzell's book provides a step-by-step process to accomplish this important task (4–7).

Build an Influence Bank

With an understanding of your power bases and a knowledge of who you are most dependent on for success, you can begin to build an influence bank by looking for opportunities to develop or strengthen a relationship with these people. This is necessary to function as a curriculum partner.

- Actively listen to their ideas and concerns, and help them achieve their goals. Build good will with and be responsive to others; never be offensive, and never make an enemy regardless of the situation. Continually look for things that you can do for others that will cost you nothing (Dilenschneider, 1990, 12, 14, 17).
- Talk regularly with the people in the organization who informally gather and dispense information. You will learn important information.

- Develop alliances with people before you need something from them. It is more likely that when you have a need, they will supply it (Bellman, 1992, 105). Respond immediately to support these people when they have a need.
- Consult public relations resources for additional ideas. There are many excellent publications available. Deposit often into your influence bank.

Keep in mind that you cultivate relationships today with the people on whom you are most dependent, for what you, they, or the organization may need tomorrow or in the future (Bellman, 1992, 105). You never know what position these people may hold in the hierarchy tomorrow and how they can impact your ability to be successful.

Library media specialists are often isolated from the rest of the learning community within the school. The library media center is frequently located on the main corridor of the school, physically removed from classroom areas. In addition, the fact that there is generally only one library media specialist in the school makes it difficult to find time during the day to collaborate with teachers on curricular issues. Therefore it is important to spend time in school activities outside the formal library that will carry over into the library media center, helping to establish rapport with your peers. This will also allow them to see you in a different light and, for some teachers, interact with you for the first time. They may find that you have special skills and talents; that you are a creative, competent person who exhibits initiative; that you have some of the same interests they do; that you play a unique and valuable role in the educational program and are trusting and trustworthy; that you are dependable.

Spending time outside the library increases the amount of time that you may be able to share ideas about the library media center and its contributions to the instructional program in an informal setting, thereby decreasing your isolation. This will help people know who you are and what you do, as well as become aware of the value of the library media program to their success (Hartzell, 1994, 6). This adds to your influence bank, which should include administrators, teachers, students, parents, and members of the larger learning community as well as the political arena. Such activity also builds your advocacy network.

Consider Your Political Self

The last step in developing influence with others is to consider the politics of the organization. You may have your own frame of reference concerning politics based on past experience and observations of the larger political sphere. You may feel that politics are in conflict with your principles. You may even believe that your school or district is not political. However, it is important to understand that politics operates in every organization. If you ignore the politics in your school and district, you will not be able to influence change when it occurs and, therefore, will become ineffective. It is essential to understand the "art of getting things done" (Bellman, 1992, 75, 76). You must learn how to work in a political setting and at the level you are comfortable, so that you can influence the outcome of the organization.

Bellman offers excellent suggestions to integrate politics within personal principles. First, know what your principles are and consider them often; know what you believe and be willing to support it. Second, accept that politics are "alive and well" in your school district, and endeavor to understand them. Third, understand that you are a part of the political process whether you choose to "play" or not. Those who do play will exclude the nonplayer from the game. Fourth, recognize that when you develop an important vision and try to share it with others, it will be considered politically as well as objectively. In developing a vision, consider both (1) the support required to have the vision become a shared one, and (2) what will happen if support for the vision is not forthcoming. Consider the ramifications as you decide how to function politically. Bellman's last suggestion comes back full circle to personal principles. The level of your participation in the politics of an organization is dependent on your self, based on observations of the organization, the experiences of others, and your own good judgment (78–79).

If you choose not to participate in organizational politics, you will probably lose the ability to influence the decisionmaking process and, therefore, lose the opportunity to ensure that students will be information literate as well as lifelong learners. As schools continue to restructure, there will be changes that directly impact your job and interests. Accept the challenge to consider your political self as you assess each situation and determine if and how you will influence it.

Although you are in a position of helping others, you can influence the learning environment and become a leader in the learning community. If you develop power bases from which to exert influence, formulate a plan of action to influence people on whom you are most dependent, create an influence bank that will enable you to accomplish your goals, and establish a level of interaction in the politics of your organization that is supported by your principles, you will successfully lead from the middle.

DECIDE TO BECOME A LEADER

Traditionally, library media specialists have been known for their excellent managerial skills and for their well-organized and well-functioning library media centers. However, they have not always been leaders. According to Warren Bennis (1989), managers administer whereas leaders innovate; managers maintain whereas leaders develop; managers focus on systems and structures whereas leaders focus on people; managers rely on control whereas leaders inspire trust; managers have a short-range view whereas leaders have a long-range perspective; managers imitate whereas leaders originate; managers accept the status quo whereas leaders challenge it; managers do things right whereas leaders do the right thing (45). In order to function as a curriculum partner, you must become a leader.

Leading begins with you. Your attitude and thinking determine your behaviors and actions. Leading is based first on a belief in yourself, by knowing that you are a leader; then on the people with whom you work, by knowing that they are open and receptive to change; next on your profession, by knowing that it has provided you with ideas, concepts, and opportunities to continue learning from which to begin to develop a vision; and finally, on the system, by knowing that it will respond to change in a positive manner (Bellman, 1992, 18). Identify a situation (problem) that you feel needs to be changed. Develop a vision that describes the situation after the change has been implemented. Start from a positive perspective and communicate that vision to others; as they discuss in turn the vision with others, it will become a shared vision that they will subscribe to and make their own. The clearer the vision is to yourself, the better you will be able to communicate it to others, the greater the possibility that you will draw people to it and that they will integrate it and follow. The people who accept this vision must believe in your ability to move them toward achieving it as well as in their own ability to contribute.

Only you can decide to step forward, become a leader, and use your leadership skills more consistently. You have an important role in helping schools develop and achieve their goals. Although it will take energy and initiative, it is absolutely necessary that you do so. You need to become a full partner with teachers in the instructional program, a curriculum partner, so that students will become information literate and capable of meeting the challenges of the future. You must have a vision of what the library media as well as the instructional program might be and have the skills to translate that vision into practice.

A SPECIAL STORY

When we are confident in our abilities and people trust us and value our ideas, we are able to model these skills and share them when working with students—trusting, supporting, and valuing them as individuals. We can empower students to be leaders. What follows is a special story of how a library media specialist, a curriculum partner and leader, did just that. Cheryl M. Krug, library media specialist at K. E. Taylor Elementary School (a K–5 school of approximately 1,350 students) of Lawrenceville, Georgia, in the Gwinnett County Public Schools tells her story:

Each day, the Taylor family begins our school day together via a live broadcast that fifth grade students produce and perform. As library media specialist, I have the unique opportunity to train these students to work as team members in producing a morning news show we affectionately call Wolf Watch. I do not touch a button or signal a reporter. All jobs are done by students, including video mixing, tape operating, audio mixing, directing, shooting, and performing. And, at the end of each broadcast, the crew and I have a team meeting, where we debrief using a quality tool known as Plus/Delta. This tool allows crew members to state what they feel went well during the broadcast as well as areas they feel they can improve.

One morning, the 9:00 bell rang, and the crew filed into the video production room to begin their ten-minute warmup and practice before the 9:10 bell that signals the start of the show and the school day. I happened to be in a grade level meeting with my administrators; the meeting was in the media center. However, the conversation was nowhere near being complete at 9:00. So, I simply signaled with a nod of my head for the students to go ahead and begin the warmup without me. The 9:10 bell rang, and as our administrators were finishing their final statements, all of us were shocked to hear the opening music signaling the start of the show. My colleagues later told me that they were surprised that I did not get up and rush into the studio. Yet, something told me to stay outside and watch the broadcast from the media center television. So, I did! And I must admit, tears welled in my eyes with pride, as I watched a crew of twelve fifth grade students perform to their greatest ability, with not one adult in the room. They produced a Wolf Watch that was second to none, and it was all due to their leadership and their pride in their performance and program. Those students were trusted and respected and given an opportunity to lead, both in the classroom and in the media program. They did so with ease and at a level of assurance and comfort that still amazes me to this day. (Cheryl Krug, personal communication, February 10, 1999)

This is the ultimate example of a successful student-centered library media program and a library media specialist who is a curriculum partner. As curriculum partner, Cheryl promoted student interest and ability in producing a daily video news program and provided necessary skills for the students to be able to complete the task. She trusted and respected each student, and they responded by learning, analyzing, creating, and producing a news program using critical thinking, decisionmaking, and problem-solving skills. When presented with an opportunity, the students felt empowered and were able to demonstrate mastery of the skills but, more important, to demonstrate that they were leaders, capable of meeting the challenges of that morning as well as of the future.

WHAT CAN I DO TO BECOME A LEADER OR TO
SHARPEN MY SKILLS TO BECOME A BETTER LEADER?

- Learn the characteristics or skills of leadership, and assimilate these into your being. Become a person who is excited about learning and is always learning; who regularly has a vision that you share with others, drawing people to this vision.

- Recognize that teacher leaders are leading from the middle and that you, as a teacher, can also lead from the middle.

- Accept the fact that your success is dependent on the success of others.

- Determine who you depend on for your success as a library media specialist— the degree of dependence and the importance of improving your relationship; and create an action plan for each person.

- Create an influence bank so that when you have a need, you have something on which to draw.

- Commit to making one change within the next three months. Identify a problem that affects others, and develop a vision by using the information presented in the Inspiring a Vision section in this chapter.

- Use leadership skills and demonstrate a passion about students and the library media program to counsel people into the library media profession who are enthusiastic about learning and are change agents in their present situation. The process of change and change agents will be discussed in chapter 3.

- Be a mentor to a new library media specialist or a library media specialist who is working to implement change. Create in that person the same energy and passion for program that you have.

- Become involved in a variety of activities in the school and outside of the media center; demonstrate in a variety of ways that you are a leader.

- Recognize that your school is a political organization, and find the level of participation that fits your principles.

- Take a leadership position in the school. You already interact with all students, with all teachers, and within all areas of the curriculum. Be open to new ideas and tolerant of all points of view (Herrin, Pointon, & Russell, 1986, 86).

- Make a long-range commitment to write a program proposal to present at a nonlibrary professional conference, or write an article to be submitted to a nonlibrary professional journal about some aspect of library media programming. Do anything you can to help change others' perceptions of the role of the library media program.

- Be a risk-taker and become a leader.

A Partnership with the Principal: Redefining Support for the Library Media Program

2

The single most important element in the development of an effective library media program is the principal (Haycock, 1990, 48). The degree to which the principal understands and supports the library media program is the degree to which that program will become the center of the instructional program, the library media specialist will become a curriculum partner, and students will have the necessary skills to function successfully in the 21st century.

PRESENT LEVEL OF SUPPORT BY THE PRINCIPAL

Although research indicates that an effective principal demonstrates both administrative as well as instructional leadership (Achilles, 1987, 20) and can have a powerful impact on the implementation of any change, the principal frequently does not exercise this leadership (Fullan, 1991, 76). Research additionally substantiates the fact that projects and programs that have the active support of the principal are more successful than those without that support. Furthermore, research and practice reveal that principals often do not have an understanding of or appreciation for the importance of the library media program. Thus it is possible that library media specialists who have a vision to share with their principal concerning the library media program may encounter a lack of interest in, understanding of, or support for the program.

The fact that the principal lacks an understanding of the library media program is not the fault of the principal but of the graduate principal-preparatory programs. Textbooks on administrator preparation, as well as course content, include little information about the library media pro-

gram or the library media specialist and their contributions to the instructional program. In a survey conducted in 1996 by Wilson and
MacNeil, more than 75 percent of the 250 graduate principal-preparatory
programs, nationwide, reported that they did not address school libraries
in their programs. Only 18 percent answered in the affirmative. Although
several programs included information on facility planning, budgeting,
and the role of the library media specialist, others indicated that their
courses were full and that although libraries were important there was
little time available for more topics to be added (Wilson & MacNeil, 1998,
115).

In addition, these administrators may remember library programs
from their own school years and regard the library as a repository of
books and the librarian as the dispenser of those books. Moreover, the
experiences during their professional careers may have been with librarians who functioned only as information specialists, spending their time
being the "keepers of books" and providing little support to the instructional program. Finally, some library media specialists may not have
altered their philosophy in response to the redefinition of their roles and
may have withdrawn to perform only those tasks that they feel are comfortable and safe. They may be overwhelmed by the present job description and believe they cannot take on any more. One principal commented
that he formed his vision for the library media program by observing
library media specialists and determining what he did not want in a
library media program.

Instead of lamenting the lack of understanding and support, it is useful
to gain an appreciation for the breadth of the principal's responsibilities
and for the daily administration of the school. Principals are expected to
function in many roles: as instructional leader, facilitator, counselor, pur-
veyor of information, business administrator, building safety coordinator, and contract administrator, to name just a few. Understanding and
being sensitive to their frustrations by showing empathy will promote a
better working relationship. Supporting the principal in his or her work
is the first step in the library media specialist's half of the partnership.

WHY IS THE PRINCIPAL IMPORTANT TO THE MEDIA CENTER?

Having a good working relationship with the principal, founded on
trust and competence, is important for several reasons. First, the principal establishes priorities and determines general policy as well as the
distribution of instructional funds. Second, the principal determines or
impacts the decision on whether the building "needs" a library media
specialist or what percentage of time is needed. Third, the principal iden-

tifies what is important, which is then supported and implemented. Fourth, the principal determines student access to the library media center, establishing whether the center will be a dynamic part of the school's instructional program or a rarely used room in the school. The following example indicates why it is important to have the understanding and support of the principal. (As author of this book, I offer this example from my own experience.)

On the first day of my first position as a two-day-per-week librarian in the early 1960s, I was invited to the school office and told by the principal (who had his back to me and was looking out the window) that he had never before worked with a school librarian or had any idea what a librarian did, and that I would need to prove to him why it was important to have a librarian in an elementary school. I was then dismissed. The meeting took no more than 30 seconds. I left feeling very inadequate and more than a little insecure. I had just graduated from college and was full of great ideas but found that I had eight classes per day, bus duty at both ends of the day as well as lunch duty in the middle, and collections in two schools that needed to be organized—or, more correctly, drastically weeded. There were sixteen classes in each of the schools, which meant that I worked with classes only every other week. I tried to "plan" with the teachers in grades K–6 for the program I presented on an alternate week basis, meeting with those teachers whose classes I would see the following week. These teachers had no idea why they should share with me what they were covering in the curriculum but did so out of courtesy and, probably, a great amount of curiosity.

Because I worked at two schools, the resources from both were available to all teachers via my courier service. My routine involved providing resources to teachers to support their curriculum; teaching library skills by using the topic the teacher was studying in social studies or science as the vehicle by which to deliver the instruction; and regularly directing articles to the principal found in the library literature about library programming, including flexible scheduling and other topics. Many days I wondered how I could do all that was required in a situation where demands were growing at a rapid rate from children and teachers who had never before had the services of a school librarian. The principal was very visible and stopped in the library several times each day. Teachers began to willingly share topics they were teaching. A few even sought me out to request specific resources. The principal was invited to the library several times each year for special projects conducted with specific classes. There were also a few opportunities to discuss program accomplishments as well as new ideas and to ask about the articles I had shared with him.

Some six years later this principal was selected to open a new grade school (K–6), and I became the librarian. In developing the program for this school, he told me he had decided that the library program would be flexibly scheduled for grades 4–6; that he was initiating teacher-librarian planning so that specific learning situations could be planned for the students within the context of their curriculum; and that grades K–3 would have a regularly scheduled class on an alternate week basis with the teacher accompanying and assisting children in the library. On the week the class was not scheduled with the librarian, the teacher was expected to bring the class to the library and conduct a planned program. I also worked with the teacher and students on the lesson or activity that the teacher planned. The library period ceased to be a planning period for teachers. The library media program became an integral element of the instructional program in that school and remained that way for the duration of this principal's tenure in that building, for twenty-five years.

This principal and I forged a partnership. He was a very special person—a visionary and an exemplary administrator. He was receptive to new ideas, respected by all with whom he worked, and interested in providing the highest level of educational programming for his students. He also convinced principals to initiate flexible scheduling in the other elementary schools in the district. This provided an impetus for other librarians to get out of the library and become involved in the instructional program.

HOW DO PRINCIPALS PERCEIVE
THE SCHOOL LIBRARY MEDIA SPECIALIST?

To develop an effective library media program and forge a partnership with the principal, library media specialists must understand how the major player in this program perceives the role of the library media specialist. In a survey conducted in the mid-1990s by Dorrell and Lawson (1995), the authors found that principals were generally more supportive of the concept of a library media center than they were about the specific library media center in their school. Furthermore, they felt that selecting resources, providing reference service to students, and generally managing the library media center were most important. They considered curriculum planning and holding conferences with teachers of only average importance. They did not provide strong support for the library media specialist as a teacher, nor did they feel it was necessary for the library media specialist to have classroom experience (78, 79). Dorrell and Lawson concluded that principals held a traditional view of the library media specialist as an individual who purchases, processes, and circulates books—as the "keeper of the books" (Olson, 1996, 12).

In a survey conducted by DeGroff (1997), administrators placed a high value on all three roles of the library media specialist as defined in *In-*

formation Power: Guidelines for School Library Media Programs (AASL & AECT, 1988)—information specialist, teacher, and instructional consultant—but they consistenly placed a higher value on the role of information specialist. DeGroff suggested (1) selecting, organizing, and using resources as well as supporting flexible scheduling as examples of the information specialist role; (2) teaching how to select and use information, promoting and supporting critical reading and thinking skills, and teaching an appreciation for the freedom of information as examples of the teacher role; and (3) participating in designing literacy curriculum and instructional strategies, ensuring that information skills are integrated in content areas, and participating in developing, implementing, and assessing unit plans as examples of the instructional consultant role. Whereas administrators reported that library media specialists were regularly functioning in teacher and information specialist roles, they were less likely to function in the role of instructional consultant (9–11, 13, 18).

These two research studies, which provide a grades K–12 perspective nationwide, indicate that principals view the library media specialist as an individual who purchases, processes, and circulates books. The studies also show a great difference between (1) their perceptions of the role of library media specialist, and (2) the expectations of the school library media specialist as well as what was advocated by *Information Power: Guidelines for School Library Media Programs*. It is unfortunate that many principals still hold these perceptions. If the roles of teacher and instructional consultant (or instructional partner, as this role has been redefined in *Information Power: Building Partnerships for Learning*; AASL & AECT, 1998) are to be implemented, the partnership between the principal and the library media specialist must become a reality.

HOW DO LIBRARY MEDIA
SPECIALISTS PERCEIVE THEMSELVES?

Library media specialists must examine the perceptions they hold of themselves. The survey conducted by DeGroff (1997) found that although library media specialists placed a high value on all three roles described in the 1988 AASL and AECT guidelines, they were less likely to practice the role of instructional consultant. Furthermore, when they attempted to practice this role, they were more likely to participate in (1) designing literacy curriculum and instructional strategies, integrating information skills in content areas, and gathering books and other resources than (2) developing, implementing, and assessing these experiences (12, 18).

Library media specialists must have a clear understanding of the role they will perform so they can discuss this with their administrator and then reinforce their words with actions. Administrators and teachers will continue to see us only in the support role that we have played in the past as long as we are satisfied to participate at this low level of involvement in the instructional program. We must change our perception of ourselves. As we do so, we will change principals' and teachers' perception of us as well.

THE PRINCIPAL AND LIBRARY
MEDIA SPECIALIST: A PARTNERSHIP

This partnership is practical because both the principal and library media specialist have several responsibilities in common. For example, they are the only people in the building who work with all teachers and all students in all curricular areas and for as long as they are in the building; further, they both manage a budget and are concerned that limited resources be shared equitably across all curricular areas. Of paramount importance is that this partnership can be a model for the supportive partnering that teachers and library media specialists require (Breivik & Senn, 1993, 26).

Granted, it would be advantageous if principals learned about the library media specialist and program in their principal-preparatory programs. Such content is seriously lacking, and the university library media programs and the library media profession at large must move more aggressively to address it. Wilson and MacNeil (1998) have created a plan that supplies a curriculum for principal-preparation courses at the graduate level made up of components integrated across coursework. For example, the school library media component in the finance course concentrates on the library media budget. There is a different component for each course. As principal-preparatory programs integrate library media programs into their curriculum, principals will enter their professional careers with critical information about the library media program. Because this will be a slow process, Wilson and McNeil have identified tasks that library media specialists who are in close proximity to one of the principal-preparatory schools can perform to help in this endeavor. Their plan suggests that library media specialists encourage professors in schools of education to include components of library media management in principal-preparation courses; volunteer to lecture for one of these classes about the role of the library media program and other library media topics; suggest that principals visit their library media center as a site during internship programs; and introduce these professors to *Information Power: Building Partnerships for Learning* (AASL & AECT, 1998, 116).

Until this takes place, you must rely on "on the job training" that only you can provide. You are the most important person in changing the perceptions of others and in developing advocacy for your program. You must know yourself and evaluate your present philosophy and program in light of *Information Power: Building Partnerships for Learning*, have a clear definition of the roles you will perform, and make a commitment to function in the roles defined therein. Using your leadership skills, embark on a plan to provide "on the job training" for your principal. This is a wonderful opportunity. Library media specialists, as a group, must take up this challenge, speak with a unified voice, and persevere until we have fulfilled the vision in *Information Power* (1998).

An Exemplary Partnership

Faye Kimsey-Pharr, principal, and Jo Ann Everett, library media specialist, Lakeside Elementary School (a grade K–5 school with 540 students and a participant in the Library Power initiative in Chattanooga, Tennessee) have created an exemplary partnership. As a result, students have benefited greatly. Jo Ann Everett shares this story:

Faye's transformation into an outstanding administrative leader began when she realized that teachers were assigning, not teaching; that test scores were declining; that children were not learning on their own because they did not have the tools; that the mountains of workbooks, worksheets, and textbooks amounted to meaningless work for both students and teachers. I gave her a copy of *Information Power: Guidelines for School Library Media Programs*. When she finished reading, she realized that its focus was school reform, not library reform. Faye began by expecting every teacher to develop at least three collaborative units with me during the year, based on the curriculum and outstanding children's literature. The library media center became flexibly scheduled as well, allowing both students and teachers to use the center at their point of need.

A lot of discussion ensued. Teachers resisted, questioned, and wanted to isolate themselves. But Faye's philosophy provided both focus and high expectation for every teacher: "You can run, but you cannot hide. This is the most effective program for kids, so we're doing it. We'll work through the problems together."

Gradually, through Faye's leadership, teachers began to try developing this new kind of unit. Successful units at each grade level helped teachers turn the corner. A few teachers acted as a stabilizing force. Teachers began talking school and library-reform ideas to each other and to parents.

Faye can be judged as an administrator not just by her efforts, but also by her results. In just three years, Mrs. Kimsey-Pharr provided the leadership that "turned the school around." Lakeside was the only elementary school in both city and county school districts to meet its expected gains and to score above the national norm in all areas. An interesting sidelight on the scores is the correlation with library usage. Teachers who made sure that their classes used the library throughout the year for research and reading had the highest scores in reference skills and reading for comprehension. These students scored as high as 95 percent mastery on the reference skills portion, proving that hands-on as well as relevant teaching is far more successful than teaching skills in isolation. The teachers who used the library the least had the lowest scores in those areas. And there was almost a one-to-one correlation between the amount of library integration/usage and the scores on certain aspects of the test. (Jo Ann Everett, personal communication, April 26, 1999)

In her own words, Faye Kimsey-Pharr proclaims:

If today's students are to be ready for the 21st century, school reformation must take place—and in a hurry! With today's vast knowledge explosion, teachers no longer can be dispensers of knowledge as they once were. Students must be taught to solve problems, think critically, and get along with others. Where are they going to learn this? Not in a classroom where desks are permanently in a row, students buried under workbooks. Quality learning will take place only where classroom teachers and library media specialists collaboratively plan units of work. In a school where reform is really happening, the library will be the most favored and the busiest place in school. Students, teachers, and parents will have open access to the library at all times. (Faye Kimsey-Pharr, personal communication, April, 26, 1999)

Faye Kimsey-Pharr and Jo Ann Everett molded a partnership that has benefited the instructional program and is evidenced in the higher academic achievement of students. Integrating some of the following ideas into your program, as well as assimilating leadership ideas described in this book, will help you develop a partnership with your principal as well.

WHAT CAN I DO TO EDUCATE MY PRINCIPAL? FORGING THE PARTNERSHIP

The plan you develop to demonstrate an effective program should include a variety of techniques to keep the principal informed. Remember that an informed person is an empowered person. If your principal knows what is happening in the library media center, he or she feels more a part of the program, has more ownership of it, and is able to discuss it knowledgeably with others. Following are some suggestions that will help to garner the support of your principal and enter into a partnership.

• Give your principal a copy of *Information Power: Building Partnership for Learning* (AASL & AECT, 1998). This will help him or her understand the concept of vision as well as the development of the library media program. When presenting the copy, point out specific chapters or concepts that you feel are important. Make sure to give your principal a reasonable amount of time to begin reading the book before engaging in a conversation about it.

- Share articles in professional journals on library media programming. Library media specialists have been able to initiate many new ideas by using this approach. This is an excellent method of educating the principal as well as giving validity to some elements of your existing program.

- Develop a strong library media program at a level where teachers are presently comfortable and at a level just above. Using Loertscher's *Taxonomies of the School Library Media Program* (1988), chart out where each teacher and team is. If a teacher is only interested in receiving resources to support what she or he is doing in the classroom, support that need and then begin to move the person to the next level, where you promote an individualized instruction philosophy with the library media program. Turner's *Helping Teachers Teach* (1993) is another resource to assist you in developing a strong library media program. Teachers will appreciate the assistance offered at the level where they are presently functioning and will share that with other teachers and, perhaps, the principal. Ultimately, the goal is to integrate information literacy standards into all areas of the curriculum by working with one teacher or team and principal at a time.

- Suggest that you both go on a field trip to a school library media center that mirrors the type or element of program you envision for your school's media center. Being able to observe the library media center in action and talk with both the media specialist and principal can provide a compelling experience in your principal's library media education.

- Make an appointment on an occasional basis (perhaps once a month) to discuss the progress of the library media program and to share its positive aspects. Because both you and the principal are busy people, it is difficult to schedule conference time. Patricia Kolencik (1998), library media specialist at North Clarion High School, Tionesta, Pennsylvania, suggests a unique communication tool: a librarian-administrator survey prepared by the library media specialist and completed by the administrator. The principal responds by circling "SA = Strongly Agree, A = Agree, N = No Opinion, D = Disagree, SD = Strongly Disagree." Following are sample statements included in Kolencik's survey (15): "The library is visible and is promoted adequately." "The library services reach out to actively serve students and faculty." "The school library program is an integral part of our total educational program." "What areas of the current library program concern you? Why?" There should be a cover letter to explain the survey as well as a short meeting to discuss the results. Kolencik stresses that this is not intended to be an evaluation tool. However, it provides a great opportunity to focus the attention of the principal on activity in the library media center (14, 15).

Peter J. Genco is the library media specialist and technology team leader at Fairview High School (a suburban school of 540 students) in Fairview, Pennsylvania. After the principal who initially hired Peter left the school to accept a new position, Peter began working with a new principal. He continues:

This individual thought that because I asked so many questions, I needed instruction on the policies and operations of the district. Some people may "wait and see." I feel I need to speak up. The principal decided to schedule a half-hour appointment each week in order to do this. As it turned out, I was able to use this half hour to instruct him on the library media program. I feel this was the most important quality time I have ever had with a principal. He became a staunch supporter of the media center program. Also during that first year a mentor was assigned to me, which is a policy of the district. Within the next few years, this mentor became the administrator in the high school. We had developed an excellent rapport during the mentoring year so that when he became the principal, he had an excellent understanding of the mission and goals of the library media program at Fairview High. (Peter Genco, personal communication, August 31, 1999)

- Invite your principal to be a participant in an activity as part of the library media program. For example, if a speaker attends a special program in your media center, ask the principal to introduce him or her. If students are culminating a book-writing project, invite the principal to present certificates. If students are presenting oral reports, invite him or her to stop in and listen to several of them. If students have produced a video as part of a project, ask the principal to view it with the rest of the class and congratulate them on their effort. You can also invite the principal to visit the library media center to see new resources and equipment.

- Develop a plan for your library media center, short range as well as long term. The depth of this plan will be dependent on your experience in the school and the rapport you have established with the learning community. If you are new to a school, you may create your own goals and objectives by using *Information Power* (1998) as a resource and share them with the principal. If you have been in the building for a year or more, you should conduct a needs assessment with the teaching staff, create goals and objectives from the information, and share these with the principal and staff. For further details see Chapter 4 of this book, Vision, Mission, Goals, and Objectives: Redefining Planning.

- Present a monthly, bimonthly, or semi-annual report to the principal. It should be concise, easy to read, and relevant. It should include a listing of (1) curricular projects or authentic learning experiences collaboratively planned, highlighting specific teachers or teams and noting your involvement either as a gatherer of resources or as a curriculum partner in the development, implementation, and assessment of a curriculum project; (2) special activities that took place in the library media center such as reading incentive programs and other public relations activities; (3) your committee work and other in-school activities as well as professional activities outside of school; and (4) statistics such as number of classes taught, number of students using the media center, number of booktalks or story-hours presented, resources circulated, and resources processed. If your library media center is flexibly scheduled, it is important to include the names of all teachers with whom you collaborated and the curricular projects that resulted, including how students came to the library—formally and informally, and an approximate amount of time students spent in the library media center completing the project.

You may feel that this report will take too much time to prepare. It may at first. However, once you begin to do this reporting, you will develop a format and establish a routine using your plan book as the source of information. The report serves as a wonderful public relations tool as well. Cynthia K. Dobrez and Lynn M. Rutan (1996), library media specialists at West Ottawa Middle School in Holland, Michigan, provide an overview of their report. They also forward a copy of the report (with all flyers that were sent to teachers concerning special programs) to people outside the school building such as the superintendent, assistant superintendents for curriculum and finance, and technology and staff development directors. The one hour each month it takes to complete the form has had positive results. Dobrey and Rutan feel it is the most important thing they do to promote their library media program (15).

- Present an annual report to the principal including an evaluation of your goals and objectives as well as a summary of the past year's curricular projects; special activities; school activities in which you participated as well as professional activities outside of school; and statistics. This report should also include an overview of your collection development plan and budget allocation for this purpose; and an evaluation of your present-year goals and objectives, results from needs assessment, and a listing of goals and objectives for the coming year. The time you invest in preparing an annual report will provide you with excellent public relations. Not only will the principal have a better understanding of the breadth of activity in process in the media center, but you will have the opportunity to share your accomplishments as well as identify your needs. Even if you do not submit monthly reports, it is critical that you submit an annual report.

- Submit your plan book regularly, as do all other teachers, and be certain to include all activity. The plan book becomes a schedule for the activity that takes place in the library media center, reflecting both student as well as teacher use. Keep in mind that the plan book cannot take the place of a monthly or bi-monthly report. This report shows your interest and initiative in program and is another demonstration of your competence. In addition to the plan book, there should be a portfolio of plans collaboratively developed by teachers and yourself as well as plans you have developed for activities that you initiated. This too will communicate your competence and expertise to the principal.

- Know what is important to the principal. Try to integrate his or her instructional agenda and vision into the library media program. For example, if the site-based decisionmaking team is working on the concept of scheduling or attendance problems, do an ERIC search on the Internet and present the principal with articles that will help the team make decisions. If the principal is on the technology committee for the district, do a search on topics such as digital electronics, telecommunications, or hypertechnologies. Send copies of articles that will support his need or interest. The key is to provide information that he needs to be successful or that is important to him.

- Create a busy and productive library media program. Demonstrate your management skills on a daily basis. Regardless of the amount of activity, the principal will be most interested in the quality of student learning that is taking place. The library media center must be well organized and smoothly operating where students are actively involved in their learning.

- Ask to be included in department chair or grade-level meetings, as a member of the administrative team, and as department chair of the library media department. If you do not have this status yet, you should request it. This interaction will help broaden the teachers' perspective of your role.

- Demonstrate leadership skills within your school. Volunteer to serve on or be elected to schoolwide committees such as the site-based decisionmaking team or leadership team. These teams are critical because in many schools they constitute the model being used to restructure the instructional program. The library media specialist is an excellent candidate for membership on this team. She or he (1) works collaboratively with all teachers and students in the school, serving the instructional needs of all ability and grade levels as well as curricular areas, and can therefore view the curriculum from a broad perspective; (2) understands the use of technology in both teaching and learning; (3) shares decision making as a partner in instruction, program, budgeting, and collection development; (4) provides information and relevant research to assist the staff to make informed choices; and (5) accesses a broad collection of information resources that extends beyond the school setting, ensuring that the teachers can concentrate on teaching rather than spending time locating materials for the committee (AASL, n.d., 1).

- Offer to design and deliver staff development programs on topics such as technology for teachers and other staff members. Include the principal and other administrators as well.

- Demonstrate your leadership skills at the district level and within the larger learning community. Volunteer to serve on districtwide committees for professional development, technology, standards, and/or reading. As you display your expertise and leadership skills at the district level, you will be asked to participate in other initiatives that will in turn enable you to influence people in the larger learning community; in this way you can promote a better understanding of the importance of school library media programs and their contributions to the instructional program. You are building your influence bank.

- Compliment your principal often on every evidence of support for the library media program. Remember that in a partnership, support flows both ways. Be sure that you also praise the principal's achievements within the school and in the larger learning community as well as offer your assistance and support as needed. Celebrate the growth of the library media program as an integral component of the instructional program.

WHAT CAN THE PRINCIPAL DO TO SUPPORT THE LIBRARY MEDIA PROGRAM? HIS OR HER HALF OF THE PARTNERSHIP

Every library media specialist has a vision of the perfect principal. Following are ideas of what the principal can do to support the library media program. You may find an opportunity to share some of these ideas. The principal in the restructured school must be the instructional leader who implements these actions.

- Develop an understanding of and appreciation for the library media program and its contributions to the instructional program; provide needed staff and resources to implement this program.

- Spend time with teachers discussing the importance of the program and how it will strengthen their instructional programs. In the words of Dr. Peter Tamburro, deputy superintendent of the Oneida City School District, a small city school district in New York State: "The support for any program begins with attitude. As an administrative staff, we must convey to staff that the library and the library media specialist are an integral part of teaching and learning. Once this is established, we must provide resources needed to meet the diverse needs of a student and teacher population. One must first be certain that the facility and staff are prepared for this role" (Peter Tamburro, personal communication, December 8, 1998).

- Create an educational climate that is focused on student learning and encourages innovation, experimentation, collaboration, and risk taking. In this atmosphere library media specialists and teachers will be more willing to demonstrate leadership and more open to change.

- Promote the role of the library media specialist as curriculum partner with the teaching staff by encouraging as well as expecting teachers and library media specialists to work collaboratively to create, implement, and assess curriculum projects, and to integrate information literacy into all curricular areas.

- Find reasons to discuss the library media program at staff, parent, administrative, and Board of Education meetings; provide opportunities for the library media specialist to speak at these meetings.

- Provide support staff to relieve the library media specialist from nonprofessional duties in the media center.

- Include the library media specialist in grade-level and departmental planning meetings on a regular basis (monthly or every six weeks). This sends a message to the learning community that the library media program is important to the instructional program. Thereafter, when flexible scheduling and collaborative planning are introduced, teachers will already understand the importance of the program and will be responsive to the change.

- Support flexible scheduling in elementary library media centers by providing alternative coverage for teachers' planning period so that teachers and students can be met at their point of need.

- Help the library media specialist become visible. Gary Hartzell, associate professor of educational administration at the University of Nebraska, Omaha, offers the following suggestions to help in this regard: "Make the status of the library media specialist equal to a department chair and team leader. Include the library media specialist in curriculum, policy, change management, and other meetings as well as in school projects to provide exposure to other teachers and administrators. Experience is built as the teacher understands how the library media specialist can assist him or her and as the library media specialist is viewed as an important resource. Rely on the library media specialist for research information, and acknowledge its source" (Gary Hartzell, personal communication, October 20, 1998).

• Encourage collaboration by providing time for teachers to plan with the library media specialist and gain confidence in sharing students as well as teaching styles. Carol Cribbet-Bell, library media specialist at Carrillo Magnet School, a participant in the Library Power initiative, Tucson Unified School District, Tucson, Arizona, shares this idea: "'Collaboration Days' are provided at the Carrillo Magnet School four times per year (one before each new grading period). The principal arranges for three substitute teachers to cover the classrooms. Teachers sign up for a half-hour time slot and indicate with whom they wish to meet. The meeting may include the art teacher, music teacher, curriculum specialist, other teachers, and myself. This is an initial curriculum conversation and sets the stage for the planning and gathering of resources that follow. I then meet individually with teachers to more formally plan the units of study and to review resources. These sessions usually occur after school. I complete a collaboration planning form after the meeting and share it with the teacher. This procedure has been very supportive of the collaboration process" (Carol Cribbet-Bell, personal communication, June 7, 1999).

• Support this collaboration by holding both teachers and the library media specialist accountable, and look for evidence of collaboration in plan books. Follow up with those individuals who do not show evidence of this collaboration (Carol Cribbet-Bell, personal communication, June 7, 1999).

• Visit the library media center often so that you know what is happening there. Then communicate your support for the library media program to staff, parents, central office, and other members of the learning community.

• Encourage and support the continuing education of the library media specialist's by providing funds (1) to attend conferences, college courses, and staff development programs; and (2) to subscribe to professional publications that will help him or her stay current, update and acquire new skills, be challenged, and grow professionally. Also provide opportunities for the library media specialist to either mentor or be mentored by another library media specialist.

• Ensure that the library media center is fully staffed at all times, and keep the media specialist's day free of outside duties such as lunch and bus supervision so that students have access to the library media center at their point of need.

• Include the library media specialist as a presenter at the orientation of new teachers. This suggestion comes from Deborah Pendleton, media coordinator, Ligon Middle School, a participant in the Library Power initiative, Raleigh, North Carolina: "Explaining the collaboration model being used in the building as well as discussing the programs and services available in the library media program at the new-teacher orientation allows us to cultivate partnerships that continue far beyond the first year" (Deborah Pendleton, personal communication, February 2, 1999).

• Review the library media program regularly, and lobby to secure funds to provide needed staff, resources, and equipment as well as allocate space for renovation as needed within the school and district.

- "Work to revise the teacher evaluation form in your district; the form should include a section on the teacher's utilization of a variety of resources, including technology, in the implementation of the curriculum. Adding this section to the evaluation form would be a great impetus toward achieving this important instructional goal" (Gary Hartzell, personal communication, October 20, 1998).

SOME FINAL THOUGHTS

Work with the principal to form a partnership, developing an understanding of the importance of the library media program within the instructional program. An understanding of roles and a change of perception between the principal and library media specialist cannot be mandated. Change comes more easily to some than to others. Principals usually become more open to change when they understand it and make it their own. This is an ongoing process; relationships and partnerships must be cultivated. It is the library media specialist who must do the reaching out. Remember, a partnership is beneficial to both partners, and each member has a responsibility to provide support and understanding to the other. Together you will redefine the library media program.

The Change Process: Redefining the Library Media Program

3

Change has had a direct impact on the philosophy and role of library media specialists for the past forty years. Our role in this process has been one of responder. This chapter addresses not only how to better respond to change but how to be an initiator of change—that is, an agent of change or change agent. With an understanding of the characteristics of change as well as an insight into how people react to it, we can successfully initiate and implement change to become a curriculum partner in the instructional program.

RESEARCH AND PRACTICE

Change takes place under various conditions: when it is imposed on us; when we become voluntary participants; or when we initiate it because we find the present situation unsatisfactory. The meaning of change is rarely understood when the change is introduced and people feel ambiguity and uncertainty throughout the process (Fullan, 1991, 31–32). It is often correlated with a sense of loss and involves struggle. Fear of the unknown is one of the main reasons for resistance to change. The people who create change are risk takers dedicated to a vision, and they take the necessary steps to implement that vision. It requires courage and resolve to create change, but the benefits to students and teachers—as well as the impact on library media programs elsewhere—are immeasurable.

What Are the Characteristics of Change?

Researchers and practitioners have identified specific characteristics of change. The library media specialist who is an agent of change must understand these characteristics when introducing any new vision or idea and must realize that they are applicable for not only the people with whom we wish to implement change but for ourselves as well.

First, change is an ongoing process rather than an event; it takes a long time and effort to internalize and put into practice. Change cannot be hurried but must be understood and, finally, accepted (Brown, Deal, & Mycio, 1998).

Second, it is an experience that is dependent on the efforts and actions of individual people. How they respond to change is very personal and may be different for each one. Some people are receptive; others are resistant (McKenzie, 1993, 86).

Third, there is a progressive sequence of change behaviors that the person with whom the change is being introduced must experience and master in order to be effective in handling the change. These behaviors are denial, resistance, exploration, and commitment. Some people move quickly through one or more of the stages and get bogged down in others; sometimes people move back to a previous stage or are unable to move on to the next (Brown, Deal, & Mycio, 1998).

Fourth, the change will be most readily assimilated if the individual feels that the change will help her do her job better. For this to occur, the change must be explained to the individual in the context that is most meaningful to her for understanding and acceptance to follow (McKenzie, 1993, 86). If the change is successful it can generate a sense of mastery, accomplishment, and professional growth (Fullan, 1991, 31–32).

Fifth, the change will be most successfully integrated if the resources to implement it are available. These resources should enable people to learn about the change, develop skills to implement it, and have ample time to integrate it as well as put it into practice within the school environment. This may require a budget line to provide sufficient funds for professional development. Lack of adequate resources is one of the main reasons that change fails.

Why Is Change Hard to Accept?

The agent of change must understand that for most people change is difficult to accept. We tend to want to keep things the way they are. When change is imposed, we strongly resent it even though we may voluntarily embrace it. We have a tendency to conform to change by changing as little as possible, by assimilating only those changes we were initially willing to try, and by fighting or disregarding the remaining aspects of the imposed change (Fullan, 1991, 35–36). We often identify with our job in terms of how well we function in it, a judgment based on our own experience or the experience of others. Change threatens to negate that experience, depriving us of the skills we have learned and the reasons for how we presently handle our job (Marris, 1975, 16). These factors must be appreciated as we embark on change for both the people who will implement it as well as for ourselves, the agents of change.

PLANNING FOR CHANGE: SCHOOL LIBRARY MEDIA MODELS

Taking into consideration the characteristics of change as well as the reasons for resistance to it, let us consider two school library media models that can be used to introduce change by library media specialists with the support of the building principal.

The Formal Model is applicable to situations in which there is extensive, broadly based change that impacts on almost everyone in the learning community. An example is flexible scheduling. The Informal Model is applicable to a situation that is less pervasive, one in which change will impact on a smaller segment of the learning community and on people who may have volunteered to participate. An example is resource-based learning or collaborative planning. These examples are not mutually exclusive. Each of the changes can be introduced to the staff as a whole or to a small number of teachers. They are used only as examples.

Formal Model

The Formal Model for change has been adapted from Susan C. Curzon's book entitled *Managing Change: A How-to-Do-It Manual for Planning, Implementing, and Evaluating Change in Libraries* (1989). There are nine steps in Curzon's change model: conceptualizing; preparing the organization; organizing the planning group; planning; deciding; managing the individual; controlling resistance; implementing; and evaluating. In the adapted change model that is incorporated in this chapter, the following steps are included: conceptualizing; discussing the project with the principal; planning team; planning process; resistance; implementation; and evaluation. (The change model has been adapted with permission of the author, Dr. Curzon.) The concept of flexible scheduling is utilized to demonstrate how change can be initiated positively through this step-by-step process. Discussion of the change process is followed by an anecdote by a library media specialist who has successfully implemented change.

Flexible Scheduling

For the library media specialist to become a curriculum partner, he or she must be available to collaborate with classroom teachers on the planning, implementation, and assessment of the instructional program. If the elementary library media specialist has regularly scheduled classes, it will be very difficult for him or her to become a curriculum partner. A flexibly scheduled program will provide time to plan with teachers as well as students, and it will ensure continued accessibility to the media center.

What is flexible scheduling? A flexibly scheduled library media center is one in which (1) the library media specialist collaboratively plans with classroom teachers to integrate information literacy standards into the context of the instructional program, and (2) teachers and students use the media center with its resources at their point of need. Although there are no regularly scheduled classes, a schedule is created at the time of planning and is continually changed as new needs arise. The schedule varies from day to day and from week to week. The teacher may schedule his class for three days in a row for two periods each day, depending on the instructional need, and then not schedule the class again for several weeks; or he may schedule the class for literature enrichment or reading groups to work directly with the library media specialist to extend a story from their literature program. Students use the library media center as a member of a class or small group, as well as individually, at their point of need. Students who wish to use the library media center individually for research or book exchange may do so at any time (Kearney, 1991, 19). This is in contrast to a regularly scheduled library media center, in which the library media specialist has a fixed schedule of classes during which information literacy standards are most likely addressed and literature activities are introduced with little or no relevance to the instructional program.

Research conducted during the past thirty years supports the importance of flexible scheduling. Tallman and Donham van Deusen (1994b) found that there is significantly less planned activity with the classroom teacher in a regularly scheduled library media center than in either the flexibly or the modified flexibly scheduled program (31). This generally means that students are learning information skills in a vacuum or outside the context of the instructional program and are not able to learn, retain, or apply the skills to other instructional settings (as do students who learn them for a specific curricular need). Tallman and Donham van Deusen (1994a) conclude that while library media specialists have regularly scheduled classes to cover planning time for teachers, there will probably be little integration of the library media program within the instructional program (37). Additionally, in research reported by Fast Facts (1998), it was found that in schools with well-staffed library media programs where library media specialists played an important instructional role with the classroom teacher, students averaged 5 to 10 points higher in reading than did those without such staffing (1, 2). For students to benefit academically in this way, the library media center must be flexibly scheduled and the library media specialist must be a curriculum partner.

Phase I: Conceptualizing

The first phase in the development of a plan for the management of change, according to Curzon (1989), is conceptualizing: considering all aspects of the project. Define the problem. Review the literature. Conduct action research. Determine if there really is a need for change. Consider both the positive and negative forces that will affect it. Identify the benefits. Consult with people who have successfully implemented the change. Reflect on the Information, dream about what the program can be, and then create an overall vision for the project with expected outcomes. Taking adequate time at this stage to conceptualize and understand the problem and the possible change will help to maximize the degree of success of the total project (26–29). This purposeful thinking and analysis are crucial to the implementation of any change.

- Before initiating flexible scheduling or any other change, it is necessary that you have already changed the perceptions of classroom teachers concerning your role as teacher, information specialist, instructional partner, and program administrator (AASL & AECT, 1998, 4–5) by demonstrating your leadership skills and competence. You may not have succeeded with every staff member, but you should have influenced a majority of them.

- As a result of reading professional literature, visiting successful flexible programs with your principal and key teachers, and taking time to reflect about your situation, you will understand the concept, know that you can be successful, and develop a list of benefits to the administrator, teachers, and students. Following are a few ideas to get you started.

    - *Benefits to administrators.* Administrators will have a restructured instructional program as a result of the restructured library media program. Flexible scheduling will allow teachers to collaborate with the library media specialist to ensure that each student is at the center of his or her learning. The staff will be more cohesive and concerned about the instructional program.

    - *Benefits to teachers.* Teachers will be able to use the library media center at their point of need—being able to schedule a class or small group, or send students individually; gain an instructional partner through planning collaboratively with the library media specialist on curricular projects or units, information skill instruction, or literature extension; have greater access to print and technology resources as the need occurs; and use the library media center as an extension of their classrooms.

    - *Benefits to students.* Students will be able to use the library media center at their point of need—being able to come as a member of a class or small group, or individually, to learn to access, evaluate, and use infor-

mation in the completion of projects and units within which information
literacy standards have been integrated; to do research on projects; and
to select resources at any time. As a result of using a wide variety of
both print and technology resources, students will become information
literate as well as technology literate.

• Often the largest stumbling block to a flexibly scheduled library media program is the absence of an alternative to providing coverage for a contractual
planning period for classroom teachers. Develop suggestions on how to cover
planning time for teachers. Suggestions might include: rotating art, music,
physical education, and any other special class on a six-day cycle; using art,
music, physical education, and any other class for four days per week with a
rotating interest group for the fifth day; increase art, music, or physical education classes to cover all planning periods of teachers (Kearney, 1991, 21).

• As you are formulating your vision—reflecting on what you have read and
seen as well as on the benefits to the instructional program—start sowing the
seeds of the concept among receptive classroom teachers and identifying possible activities that could be planned collaboratively if the library media center
were more available. Involve interested staff members in your thinking.

Phase 2: Discussing the Project with the Principal

Once the vision is clear, the library media specialist should present
this vision to the principal. By now the library media specialist and principal should have established a working relationship and developed a
mutual respect. If the principal is new to the building, it would be unfair
to bring a suggestion to initiate a broadly based change. Likewise, if the
library media specialist is new to the building, it would be rare for this
individual to successfully initiate change without having established a
working relationship with the principal and teachers. Be prepared to
answer any question and to expand on any concept. The principal must
understand precisely how the change will function, how it will affect the
present situation, and how it will impact on the achievement of students.

The principal will approve, approve with modifications, or disapprove
the vision. If she approves the project or approves it with modifications,
the library media specialist can move to the next phase of the planning
process. If the principal disapproves the project, the library media specialist must revisit the conceptualizing phase and determine if a change
is still necessary. If it is, the specialist should begin to create a vision
anew, taking into consideration the concerns of the principal.

• After much reflection, create a vision for the way in which flexible scheduling
will operate in your library media center with its attendant benefits, and present it to the principal to gain her support. If she is convinced that this will help
improve the instructional program, she will find the means to implement the
change—including providing alternative means for covering contractual planning time for teachers.

• If the principal does not approve the project, you must go back to the research, modify your vision to address the concerns of the principal, and present it again for her approval. It is not possible to go any farther without her strong support. The challenge is less daunting if you and the principal have already forged a partnership. The principal must be able to articulate the vision to the learning community and express her expectations for the program. She will be the first to hear when someone is unhappy with the program, so she must be able to discuss it logically and clearly with the teacher or parent.

Phase 3: Planning Team

After the principal has approved the project, the planning team must be formed. Curzon (1989) suggests that the team constitute between two and eight people who understand the change, are creative, and have a broad perspective. The planning team can be made up of volunteer members, the library media committee, or one teacher from each grade level or subject area. Parameters for the team's authority must be defined (will it be advisory or decisionmaking?), and the members of the team need to understand their purpose (41, 43).

One of the first agenda items should involve the library media specialist sharing the vision for the project and reviewing the background information developed during the conceptualizing phase. There should be ample time for team members to discuss these issues and make modifications. Although the library media specialist has done the preliminary thinking, it is now the responsibility of the team to plan the final project (Curzon, 1989, 49, 50).

• The planning team should be composed of the principal and key members of the teaching staff as well as parents who can be influential in the implementation of flexible scheduling. If you have a Library Media Advisory Committee, this group could function as this team. This committee will be discussed in Chapter 4.

Phase 4: Planning Process

When the vision is agreed on, the planning team should generate as many options as possible to solve the problem as well as gain consensus on the options that will become a part of the final plan. Different techniques will be employed when working with different groups and problems. Each technique should be preceded by a review of the problem to be addressed, together with background information and other pertinent details. Possible techniques include: brainstorming (getting as many ideas on the table as quickly as possible with no evaluation), subgrouping (identifying subtopics and allowing individuals in a large group to form subgroups around topics of interest), and using nominal groups (everyone has an opportunity to share an idea equally with everyone else as the recorder goes around the table noting each individual's idea, which the individuals have written down in preparation). The goal of this process is to gain consensus on the options and to select the best options for the organization. Curzon's book explains these three processes as well as others.

When team members have reached consensus on options that will help them solve the problem, they must develop (and gain consensus on) goals and objectives for the project that can be easily evaluated. The goals and objectives should be discussed and agreed on by the entire team (Curzon, 1989, 58–59).

During this phase of planning, a written report including all aspects of the project should be prepared for submission to the principal, superintendent, or Board of Education. The library media specialist can most easily prepare the background information. By now the vision, goals, and objectives are complete and can be added to the background. Then the last three sections of the report must be planned: implementation, budget, and timetable. The implementation plan contains both a description of the change and an action plan of activities for its implementation. The team will need to (1) consider the costs of the project, including materials, equipment, and staff, and (2) create a timetable or schedule for approval of the project and implementation of the plan (Curzon, 1989, 60, 61). Depending on the nature of the change, this part of the process may be less formal than the earlier parts.

The project will be approved, approved with modifications, or disapproved at this level. The reasons for the decision—acceptance, modification, or rejection—should be openly shared with the planning team. Members have contributed a significant amount of time and energy to this project and should have the opportunity to express their feelings. They need to feel that the work they did is valued and appreciated. However, if the plan is not approved, members of the planning team may be reluctant to participate in other projects (Curzon, 1989, 69, 70).

- Options for the planning team are as follows: survey staff members through an informal or formal assessment tool regarding the way they presently use the library media center and how they would use it if it were more available; create modest goals and objectives as well as an action plan from this information; develop a reasonable timeline for implementing each action step; resolve any financial issues; and assist the library media specialist in talking with teachers to gain an understanding of the program.

Phase 5: Resistance

Any change, positive or negative, elicits emotions and behaviors on the part of the person receiving the information. Regardless of the change, people need to be treated with respect. The principal and library media specialist must understand that a person confronted with change experiences a sequence of feelings (Curzon, 1989, 75).

The normal response to a negative imposed change will, more than likely, be a negative response. Initially people may feel shock, fear, anger, or depression. They will either integrate the change or alienate themselves from the organization. In response to positive change the person will feel surprise, apprehension, and acceptance. It is important to keep channels of communication open and be supportive and available as individuals experiencing either positive and negative change move through these behaviors (Curzon, 1989, 75–83).

Brown, Deal, and Mycio (1998) describe the Transition Model for understanding change. They contend that most individuals will move through four phases in every negative or imposed change: denial, resistance, exploration, and commitment. People experiencing positive change usually enter this model at the exploration level. However, not all individuals move through each phase in the order given. As incremental steps of understanding are gained, individuals move to the next phase. However, in order for the individual to work effectively within the changed organization, he or she must eventually reach commitment.

Think of this model as a downward curve. At the high left side we find the present circumstance. With the introduction of change we begin moving down the side of the curve, finding denial and then resistance. Moving up the right side of the curve we find exploration and, finally, commitment. At the high right side the transition is complete

The first phase, denial, begins when people hear about the change and understand that change is imminent. Because this phase is a defense against the change, people often avoid the topic as much as possible and act as though nothing is happening. Denial is normal and predictable and sometimes even helpful.

The second phase, resistance, begins when people move beyond denial and realize how upset they are. The innovation or change becomes disruptive and personally disagreeable. Resistance can also occur after an initial acceptance, at a point when people feel discouraged or disillusioned. They show anger at the organization, believe the task is impossible, feel overwhelmed and depressed, and refuse to cooperate. At this point it is important to discuss with participants why they feel resistant to the change. A dangerous form of resistance occurs when individuals disguise their resistance and work in the background against the change. This type of behavior must be addressed openly. The leader must be a good listener, acknowledging and supporting individuals in experiencing their feelings but not trying to argue with resistance or resolve people's feelings. This is the bottom of the cycle; people at this point may move back and forth between resistance and exploration as they begin to explore the potential.

The third phase, exploration, begins when people regard the change as an opportunity and no longer a threat. People exhibit energy, want to solve problems, create a vision of the future, take risks, and generate many ideas. At this point leaders need to become facilitators, helping people develop their plans for successful change.

The fourth and final phase, commitment, is reached when people choose to accept the change. They demonstrate improved productivity, morale, enthusiasm, and a sense of purpose; they also feel comfortable and successful with the change.

- While resistance to change is normal, team members may want to discuss problems with people as they occur. Do not allow a problem to fester and spread.

Phase 6: Implementation

Curzon (1989) explains that the implementation phase moves the organization from the present method of operation to the desired state as described in the implementation plan. The timing of this phase is important. Most often, the best time is when little else in the way of change is happening in the school or school district, and the budget is solid (95–97). The change should be formally introduced by the principal or superintendent. This should not be left to a memorandum placed in teachers' mailboxes.

Curzon also suggests piloting the change or parts of the change before the full implementation process begins. The pilot should be carefully evaluated and the full implementation plan adjusted as needed (1989, 99).

Once the implementation phase is concluded, it is time to bring a close to the work of the planning team. Thank team members and any other people who were a part of the project, personally and in writing, and place a copy of the letter in each person's personnel file. Team members should feel appreciated for the good work they accomplished and the direction they provided (Curzon, 1989, 104).

- Staff development is critical for the implementation of flexible scheduling as well as for teachers to gain an understanding and comfort level with this change. Although they may have requested some resources from the library media center in the past, in many cases the main service they received was coverage during their planning period. Until now these teachers have been completely responsible for their instructional program, and they may not regard partnering with the library media specialist as a welcome change. Flexible scheduling is an entirely new way of viewing the library media center and its contributions to their classrooms and students. Teachers must go through a complete reorientation toward the library media program. This staff development may take place at the large-group, team, grade, or individual level. The large group is appropriate for a philosophical overview of the program presented by the principal showing her strong support. From this point on, working with teams or grade levels and individuals is advisable, as it enables

you to gain the best information as to their level of understanding and acceptance. A visit to successful flexible programs can also be part of staff development. Peer coaching and feedback, as well as follow-up discussions and
meetings, are imperative to stay on top of the implementation process.

- The strategies of collaborative planning, resource-based learning, and a research process for students are critical components of a flexibly scheduled library media program. Just because the library media center is now flexibly
scheduled does not mean that teachers will immediately begin to integrate the
media program into their instructional program. They need specific strategies
and techniques that will help them understand how this can be accomplished.
These components will become staff development topics as well. Collaborative
planning and resource-based learning are discussed more fully in Chapter 5 of
this book, and research processes are discussed in Chapter 6.

- Schedule classroom teachers regularly for a planning time. Keeping close contact with teachers will help you maintain the program, answer questions, and
respond to any problem. Charlotte Vlasis, library media specialist at the
Chattanooga School for the Liberal Arts (grades K–8 with 450 students) and a
participant in the Library Power initiative, in Chattanooga, Tennessee, recom-
mends, "Flexible scheduling provides opportunities for teachers to plan the use
of the library in a way that best meets the needs of their students. Planning
times are 'fixed.' Those times stay the same on the library schedule each week,
and teachers know that I will be available (and expecting) to plan with them"
(Charlotte Vlasis, personal communication, June 2, 1999). In addition, research
suggests that planning with a team of teachers is more satisfying and usually
generates more ideas than planning with individual teachers (Tallman & Donham van Deusen, 1994a, 37). Team members are energized by the ideas of other
team members. They are generally more willing to work collaboratively with
you than when planning alone. It is also advisable to keep the schedule (for
the current week and the next two weeks) in full view so that everyone has
this information.

- Make sure that all teachers and students are participating to some extent in
the library media program. Helping teachers understand how the program will
function, how they will fit into it, and how both teachers and students will
benefit are crucial to the success of the program. Collaboratively planned curricular projects or units as well as the literature program will bring teachers
and their classes (or groups or individuals) to the media center to complete
assignments. Teachers need to learn, test new ideas, reflect, discuss progress,
and then try again. However, it is critical that you have controls in place to
ensure the participation of all teachers at some level, which, in turn, will ensure
equitable access and use of the library media center by students. McGregor
(1999) has identified several barriers to flexible scheduling: size of collection,
clerical help, and how the teacher teaches. The size of the collection and the
lack of clerical help can be remedied by writing grants, asking the principal for
clerical assistance, or requesting parent volunteers. These people will provide
excellent assistance at the same time you are building an advocacy group. However, if the classroom teacher feels that students will not learn without him
teaching, special accommodations must be made to ensure that his students

will be able to use the library media center. Do not give up, however. Go back to the drawing board with the principal to derive solutions that will include the involvement of the teacher and students.

- Flexibility is key in a flexible library media program. If you want a flexible program, then you must be prepared to be very flexible yourself. You will need to be comfortable with a certain amount of disorder and disorganization—"organized confusion." Depending on the size of the media center, you may have several classes, groups, and students all using the facility and resources at the same time. You must also be prepared to be flexible in accommodating the needs of teachers. Recognize that without each teacher's involvement and support, there will be no student involvement; and without students actively using the library media center, the program will revert to regularly scheduled classes. Being flexible and having the involvement of the classroom teacher is paramount to the success of your program. Energy, persuasive powers, clear thinking, and understanding must be directed toward each teacher.
- Plan a program on flexible scheduling for parents as well. They, too, need to understand the benefits to their children in using the library media center at their point of need.
- Support staff is an important component of a successful flexibly scheduled program. If the principal is committed to this change, she will find the means to provide this assistance. Although volunteers and student assistants are no substitute for support staff, they can provide useful assistance.
- Good communication in written and spoken formats is essential in the implementation of flexible programming. There is a growing body of literature and practice on flexible scheduling that can assist and support you in making this change. *Flexible Access Library Media Programs* by Jan Buchanan (1991) is an excellent resource.

Phase 7: Evaluation

Evaluation is the last phase of the process of managing change and often is the one most neglected or ignored. The evaluation not only determines if the goals were met but also if they were not met and the reasons for this. If goals are not met or other challenges are revealed, the principal and library media specialist must make modifications in a timely manner. Depending on the scope of the challenge, the planning team may be brought back together to assist in making the modifications. The information gained from this evaluation increases the probability of successful change in the future (Curzon, 1989, 107, 110, 112).

When the project is complete, share the results with everyone involved: teachers, students, parents, superintendent, and Board of Education. This can be done by memorandum, meeting, or presentation. Now is a time of celebration—share the rewards with those who made the change successful, and celebrate their accomplishments. Of equal importance is the sharing of negative results. However, this is more difficult; it requires an open climate within the organization to allow people to take risks and possibly fail (Curzon, 1989, 114).

- The evaluation of teacher and student use of the flexible program is critical. Use records for circulation and attendance of classes, groups, and individuals; planning sessions with teachers; a careful evaluation of the goals and objectives; an informal assessment by teachers; and anecdotal information all should be included. Student achievement data should also be analyzed. Share this information regularly with the principal in your monthly report and with your staff. Library media specialists who have been successfully operating flexible programs will tell you that it takes between three and five years for a program to function properly. Begin your program slowly, using half of each day for the flexible program, focusing on just grades 3–6. In the words of a fifth grade student, "It (library time) means more now that it relates to our class work." Students who understand that the library media center is a place to go when they have an information need will see the connection to all libraries (Bernstein, 1997, 11). Ultimately the goal is to conduct a flexibly scheduled program so that all students and teachers can use the library media center at their point of need.

From a Library Media Specialist Who Implemented Change

Rebecca Camhi has been the library media specialist for the past twelve years at the Herbert Hoover Elementary School in the Kenmore—Town of Tonawanda School District, a suburban school district in Kenmore, New York. There are approximately 700 students in 33 classes in this K–5 school. At one time, there were one and one-half library positions. Recently the half-time position was eliminated. Rebecca and her principal saw the impending cut as an opportunity to change to flexible scheduling.

At that time, Rebecca was providing contractual planning time for fifteen teachers each week. Under this structured program, students came to the library media center weekly to receive information/library skills instruction or literary enrichment. They learned these skills in a vacuum with no subject-area context in which to utilize them. Because this was the planning time for teachers, they were not present in the library media center, did not know what skills were presented to students, and were unable to provide curricular activities to reinforce them.

Rebecca tells her story:

For several years, I had been reading articles in professional journals on flexible scheduling and discussing this concept with colleagues who had successfully implemented this change. I also shared these journal articles with my principal as well, discussed the concept with her, and highlighted its benefits to students. She was very receptive to the idea. I knew that for our students to become information literate, they had to learn information/library skills in the context of curricular content and then have many opportunities to practice these skills. I felt that flexible scheduling would address this problem. In considering both the positive and negative forces that would affect this concept, I determined that the greatest restraining force was the fact that I was used as contractual planning time for fifteen teachers. This meant that additional time in the schedules of special area teachers—art, music, physical education—would need to be requested.

In the spring of that year, faculty members accompanied the Library Media Advisory Committee on a visit to an elementary school that was already operating on a partial flexible schedule. Nineteen teachers as well as the principal heard the principal, library media specialist, and a classroom teacher share how the program functioned within the instructional program and its benefits to students. This group was favorably impressed with the program and agreed that if the part-time position was cut, this was a viable alternative.

I created an overall vision for the project: "Students in grades 1–5 in the Hoover Elementary School will have flexible access to their library media center as well as have skill instruction and do research at their point of need. Teachers and the library media specialist will team to collaboratively develop, implement, and assess curricular projects and activities. Students will be immersed in the topic being studied in the classroom, and the media center will be viewed as an extension of that classroom. Information/library skills will be taught as an integral part of the classroom content."

When the principal called to inform me that the part-time position had been eliminated, she recommended the implementation of flexible scheduling in September. The major restraining force had been resolved by the principal when she was able to increase the position of two special subject area teachers to cover most of the fifteen classes for which I had been responsible. At the same time the professional part-time position was eliminated, the library clerk position was increased to full-time.

On the first day of school, I distributed a menu of ideas for lesson plans spanning the curriculum entitled, "Library Media Center Ideas." It was a tool to help teachers begin to think of ways to integrate the library media program into their curriculum. My goal was to make the process as easy as possible in order to ease them into integrated instructional planning. I continue to distribute this menu of ideas each month. These lessons, which include all grade levels, are designed to cover one or more skills from their local Standards and include a broad range of topics from which to choose.

The transition was smooth. Although all these variables were in place, the principal and myself were supportive and available as teachers went through this change.

However, two years after the introduction of flexible scheduling, a small group of teachers felt that collaborative planning was too time consuming. The Library Media Advisory Committee, under the direction of the principal, met with each grade level to determine exactly what the problem was and how it could be resolved. The Advisory Committee members also pointed out that with a structured program, I prepared for six classes per week. With the flexible program, I could have thirty-three classes for which to prepare lesson plans and select resources. Teachers began to appreciate the magnitude of the flexibly scheduled program and how much more time consuming collaborative planning was for me.

There was daily planning time included in the teaching schedule from 8:00 to 8:45 before students arrived and school began. Teachers could use this time to plan with me to develop projects and learning activities. Although some of these activities would require that I only pull resources to be used in the classroom, in many of the activities I teamed with the classroom teacher and was a full teaching partner in creating, implementing, and assessing curricular units.

Evaluation of the library media program has been informal, and as problems were brought to the attention of members of the Library Media Advisory Committee, principal, or myself, they were dealt with promptly and to the satisfaction of all parties. Evaluation of all aspects of the program is a critical part of the planning process. Suggestions to improve and simplify planning were taken into consideration and implemented the following school year. These improvements continue to work. (Rebecca Camhi, personal communication, March 5, 1999)

Informal Model

The Informal Model for change, which is a modification of the Formal Model, is less structured and involves fewer people at the outset. The major difference is that the participants have volunteered to be involved in the change. Gordon Coleman (1993) describes the people involved in change as *innovators, middle adopters,* or *late adopters* (79). His explanation of these groups is used in the discussion of the Informal Model for change in the sections that follow.

Phase 1: Conceptualizing

When the library media specialist identifies a problem—such as the lack of planning for curricular projects, the inefficient use of excellent curricular resources, or the inadequate information the library media specialist has about these projects before students come to the library media center—he determines that a change is necessary. He should follow all phases in the Formal Model beginning with Phase 1: Conceptualizing.

The library media specialist has been reading about collaborative planning and feels this concept would help to improve the quality of projects; include the library media specialist in the planning, implementation, and assessment of these projects; and provide better use of resources. He has also talked with colleagues from other school districts who have already implemented collaborative planning. However, he also realizes that some teachers use only the textbook and lectures, whereas others do not wish to integrate their curriculum and still others are unwilling to share their students. These teachers would not be ready to collaborate. As part of the conceptualizing phase, the library media specialist must identify staff members who may be willing to participate in the change—teachers who have already demonstrated a willingness to plan research assignments, teachers who welcome new ideas. These are the people, according to

Coleman (1993), who are innovators. He suggests that *innovators* are looking for new ideas and strategies that will improve their instructional program. They are open to change and embrace it. They are the easiest people to persuade (79). The library media specialist should make a list of possible participants to discuss with the principal in the future. Remember that the key to this phase is to allow adequate time to understand the problem, identify the change, think about possible participants, and get a clear vision of the project. (Refer to Phase 1 of the Formal Model.)

Phase 2: Discussing the Project with the Principal

In the next phase, the library media specialist makes an appointment to speak with the principal and discuss the vision as well as the list of possible participants in an effort to get her recommendations and gain support. There is an assumption that the library media specialist has already developed a broad base of support within the school. The principal will approve, approve with modifications, or disapprove the project. (Refer to Phase 2 of the Formal Model.)

There is a difference of opinion as to whether each principal, regardless of circumstance, should be included at this point in the Informal Model. As author of this book, I hold the very strong opinion that the principal should be included in everything we do. Consider it part of her education. We want principals to feel empowered, to be knowledgeable, to have a good understanding about the program and its relationship to the instructional program, and to share this information with others. The only way to accomplish this is to use every opportunity to communicate this message clearly. Some library media specialists may say that the change is too insignificant. But I maintain that there is no change too small to involve the principal. This is another opportunity to build rapport and trust with the principal and to educate her about the multifaceted role the media center program plays in the instructional program.

There may be a principal who denies all requests because she does not understand the importance of the library media center program to the achievement of students. This is your challenge. Embark on an educational program for her and wait to initiate the change. You may say that you have learned how to work around your principal and can do it in this situation also. A word of caution: The first teacher who complains about anything that has to do with the project, when the principal has no idea what the teacher is talking about, will immediately create a very difficult, uncomfortable, and far-reaching problem for you and the library media program. The principal will become distrustful and will be less inclined to be supportive of any part of your program.

Phase 3: Organizing the Planning Team

The planning team will be made up of the teachers who have volunteered to participate in collaborative planning. You will probably chair or lead the team. Although you have done the preliminary thinking, it is now the responsibility of the team to plan the final project. (Refer to Phase 3 of the Formal Model.)

Phase 4: Planning

This phase includes creating options, evaluating them, and then choosing the best option or options; writing the goals and objectives; and developing the remainder of the plan. At this point the planning group may decide to prepare a written plan and submit it to the principal. However, in this model, sharing is generally informal. The group may request a meeting to update the principal and keep her informed. (Refer to Phase 4 of the Formal Model.)

Phase 5: Dealing with Resistance

Although the library media specialist may encounter some resistance as the project begins, because the people who are implementing the project are its creators the resistance should be minimal. These people now "own" the project and work for its successful implementation. However, it is a good idea to reread the section on resistance, Phase 5 in the Formal Model, and be supportive as people begin asking why they volunteered to participate. Be sure to celebrate the successful completion of each phase of the project, highlighting the contributions of each member.

Phase 6: Implementing

The planning team will determine the right time to launch the project, to choose to formally introduce the change to the rest of the staff or not to do so, and to work with the project until there is a sense of success. (Refer to Phase 6 of the Formal Model.)

Phase 7: Evaluating

The project should be evaluated to determine if it achieved its goals and if it should be implemented with additional teachers—and if so, who these will be. (Refer to Phase 7 of the Formal Model.)

If the change is working successfully with the innovators, the library staff may be ready to expand this concept with the middle adopters.

Phase 8: Expanding the Project

If the decision is made to expand the project, you will need to consider additional staff members who may be willing to participate in the change. These are the people, according to Coleman, who are the *middle adopters*. Coleman (1993) suggests that this represents the largest group; before they agree to participate, they must understand how the change will benefit them. Discussion with teachers in the building who are successfully implementing the change, as well as visits to their classrooms, will help persuade these middle adopters to embrace the change (79).

You should revisit Phase 1: Conceptualizing (in the section entitled Formal Model earlier in this chapter) to determine if adding people to the project affects the vision. If so, it should be re-created. Although this time around the process will be more informal, you will want to review each phase of the Informal Model so that nothing is left to chance. Remember to make the most recent members to the change process feel welcome.

Once the project is working with the middle adopters, you will want to consider the last group to be included in the project, the *late adopters*. According to Coleman, these are people who are closed-minded and difficult to convince of any new idea regardless of the benefit to them or their students. These are the last people to participate in a change (79). Depending on the project, you may choose not to include these people. However, if you choose to include this group, you may want to ask for assistance from the principal to help persuade them to participate. This is another reason to include the principal at the beginning of the project. If you move forward with this group, you should revisit the Informal Model and leave nothing to chance.

Remember that whether you are implementing a vision via the Formal or Informal Model, change takes time, is dependent on the efforts of individuals who experience a range of change behaviors, and will not be assimilated until individuals feel that the change helps them do their job more successfully. Because all students must be information literate and be able to function successfully in the 21st century, the innovators, middle adopters, and even the late adopters must all integrate the change and work collaboratively with the library media specialist to develop, implement, and assess curricular units, making the library media specialist a full curriculum partner in the instructional program.

Locally Based Research

When most library media specialists understand that there is a need for change and develop a vision for that change, their ideas come primarily from personal experience, reading journals, talking with colleagues, attending professional conferences, taking courses within their school district or at a local college, and using common sense. The library media specialists in the examples included in this chapter got their ideas from these sources. However, library media specialists can also conduct research to derive solutions to their problems.

When we think of research, we often think of experimental or large-scale change that requires a high level of expertise, demands a great amount of time to conduct, and often seems to have nothing to do with existing problems. Englert (1982) suggests that "research has only two essential elements: hard thinking and careful data gathering" (246). Therefore, when someone endeavors to learn something new by thoughtfully analyzing a problem and systematically gathering facts concerning it, he or she is conducting research (246).

Locally based research enables the library media specialist to make decisions about existing and real problems with which he is confronted. The research is very narrow and specific to his unique situation. Its goal is to solve the problem, improve this specific situation, and change existing circumstances. In conducting this type of research, the library media specialist is involved either by himself or in collaboration with an outside researcher if a specific expertise is needed. It is systematic with established methods of design, data collection, and analysis. Existing groups of students in the school are frequently used, and the results are specific to that school, to that library media center, and to those students. The results are not generalized beyond that situation. Because the library media specialist usually needs a solution to an immediate problem, the research must be concluded in a comparatively short time (Englert, 1982, 247–248).

Action research is one method of locally based research that can be used effectively. There may be a problem for which you can conduct action research right now. Is your collection adequate to support authentic learning activities in content areas? Would an analysis of your collection help justify an increase in your resource budget? Would a summary of time spent completing nonprofessional tasks convince your administrator that a support staff member is needed? Action research that involves collecting, analyzing, and reporting data concerning your library media program can help you determine how well it is performing in a specific area and provide you with documentation for the need to perform at a higher level.

Howe (1998) points out that although action research projects have been reported for classrooms as well as public and academic libraries, there have been few action research projects on school library media centers reported in the professional literature except for the July 1997 issue of *School Libraries Worldwide*. Two action research topics in this issue are "student use of the Internet" and "student survey findings on the information skills program" (30). If each of us, as library media specialists, were to conduct and report on one action research project, the research available to other library media specialists when confronted with problems would help them find satisfactory solutions. The programs we deliver to students would improve proportionately.

Library media specialists who conduct action research are leaders. Even as this research helps them function better as curriculum partners with classroom teachers, many more media specialists who are engaged in this type of research and who are agents of change are needed to lead the profession in the 21st century and redefine the library media program.

Vision, Mission, Goals, and Objectives: Redefining Planning

4

We need to know where we are going, to determine if we have arrived at our destination. We must have a practical and achievable plan to get there as well. There are many educators and managers who consider the creation of a vision statement to be the first step in the development of any program. This chapter explores planning processes that enable you to plan a library media program by developing vision and mission statements as well as goals and objectives. This approach to planning provides direction in making daily decisions as well as conducting long-range program assessment. In order to create this type of program it is assumed that you are a leader, have already developed a partnership with your principal, and are an agent of change.

The three scenarios described in the section that follows will get you started conceptualizing about the creation of a vision, mission, and goal-driven library media program. These demonstrate a progression of quality library media programming. As you read, try to identify yourself on this continuum.

PLANNING MODELS

Scenario 1

You are a new library media specialist working in this position for the first time. You have discussed the instructional program, community, and library media program with the principal. You feel fortunate to have been able to discuss the collection with the former library media specialist, in addition to generally "looking" at the collection, spot-checking copyright dates on materials, and reviewing the electronic spreadsheet of holdings for the present collection. You have talked with key people on the faculty who were recommended by the principal. After the discussion with the principal, a review of the collection, and the feedback you received from faculty members, you are prepared to select modest goals for the program. You have read *Information Power; Building Partnerships for Learning* (AASL & AECT, 1998) and decide to use goals found in this document for your new library media program. Once you have selected the goals and created objectives, you discuss them with the principal to get her suggestions for modification as well as approval. You work to achieve these goals for the remainder of the year and evaluate their progress regularly. As necessary, you adjust them with information learned as you work in this school. At the end of the school year, you evaluate each objective and share this information with the principal.

Scenario 2

You are a library media specialist who has worked in the school for at least one year. Although you have received feedback from teachers, students, administrators, and parents concerning the library media program, it has been more informal and anecdotal than objective and inclusive. You decide to broaden the base of involvement in the library media program through the use of a survey that will provide you with specific and focused data regarding the program. Once you have created the survey, you share it with the principal and then several teachers to get their feedback before asking others to respond to it. You prepare an additional survey for students to complete at each grade level. You keep these surveys short and simple. After receiving the responses, you analyze the results and prioritize areas of need. You have access to a bank of goals and objectives from which you select to match needs identified in the survey with specific goals and objectives. You also create a vision and mission statement by using *Information Power: Building Partnerships for Learning* (1998) as a foundation. You then discuss the vision and mission statements as well as the results of the survey, together with the goals and objectives you selected, with the principal to get her suggestions for modification. You see these as "works in progress" and value the principal's ideas and experience. Once this is accomplished, you share this information with the staff as well. Modeling a goals-driven program, you work to achieve these goals for the remainder of the school year and evaluate their progress regularly. At the end of the school year you assess the progress on each objective and share this information with the principal and staff. This information is also used to develop the survey of needs you will administer to members of the learning community at the beginning of the next school year.

Scenario 3

You have been the library media specialist in this building for several years and have developed a working relationship and rapport with the administration, staff, students, and parent community. You have conducted a goals-driven media program for the past two years. You have demonstrated the characteristics of a leader within your learning community and have been able to initiate changes that have benefited both teachers and students. You have developed a mutual trust and respect with the staff, who feel comfortable giving you honest, open feedback about their needs and expectations. You are positive, energetic, and flexible, and you find opportunities to celebrate the accomplishments of others. There is a good exchange of ideas, and many staff members are presently collaborating with you on curricular units to integrate information literacy standards into their content areas. You decide that it is important to further expand the base of support of and involvement in the library media program by requesting input and feedback from the staff on the creation of vision and mission statements for the library media program as well as goals and objectives. You discuss this vision with the principal and seek her support to form a library media advisory committee—a representative group that initiates this planning process and ultimately involves members of the learning community in the development of the library media program.

PLANNING YOUR LIBRARY MEDIA PROGRAM IN COLLABORATION WITH THE LEARNING COMMUNITY

In Scenario 1, the library media specialist plans the library media program with some input from selected staff members and from the principal. This input, as well as the library media specialist's evaluation of the collection, forms a basis for developing goals for the program. This is the minimum input from members of the learning community in the development of a program. In Scenario 2, the library media specialist plans the media center program as a result of an analysis and prioritization of data from a needs survey completed by administrators, teachers, and students who stand to gain from the assessment of the library media program. The media specialist develops vision and mission statements and goals and objectives. Although this is better than Scenario 1, it does not directly involve members of the learning community in the development of these building blocks of program. In Scenario 3, the library media program including the vision, mission, goals, and objectives is planned with significant feedback from members of the learning community in collaboration with the library media advisory committee, resulting in a broad base of support and ownership of the program. The library media program now "belongs" to members of the learning community.

Few if any of us exactly fit the scenarios as presented. Although many cluster within Scenarios 1 and 2, we want to move as soon as possible from (1) developing a library media program with little or no input from those for whom the program is created, to (2) developing a program with the broad base of involvement from members of the learning community as described in Scenario 3. Although these scenarios represent a continuum of improving program quality, it is critical that before moving forward to the next level you feel confident of the support of the program from both the administration as well as the staff. You must also be clear about why the change is necessary and how it will impact the instructional program.

If the library media program is viewed by staff members as the sole responsibility of the library media specialist, it will not become an integral part of their instructional program. When teachers can see how the media program is vital to their program, they will feel more ownership of it—the library media center will become an extension of their classroom, and they will want to collaborate with you to integrate information literacy standards into their content area. As a result, the instructional program will be restructured. This is accomplished by demonstrating, daily, how central the media program is to their instructional program. By involving members of the learning community, each will assume more responsibility in ensuring that all students become information literate—able to access, evaluate, and use information effectively.

Conceptualizing

Now that you have decided where you are on the continuum and that you wish to move along that continuum to broaden the base of support for and involvement in the library media program, you must identify the steps needed to move forward. This process requires research, discussion with those who have successfully implemented a planning process, and reflection. As mentioned in the previous chapter, the first step in initiating any change is conceptualizing—which includes thoroughly thinking through the idea by considering why the planning process is important; what factors will affect it both positively and negatively; what steps can be taken to implement the process; and how it will impact on the library media as well as the instructional programs. Because the goal of education is to improve student learning, you must reflect on how this planning process for the library media program will help achieve this goal. Part of conceptualizing also involves reflecting on each element of the plan—vision, mission, goals, and objectives—and identifying key concepts for both the vision and mission statements for your program. Although a planning committee will establish the planning process described in Scenario 3, it is important that you formulate a vision and mission statement from which the planning team can work. Information later in this chapter describes how to develop these components of planning. The procedures and tools described in the sections that follow will assist you to move from where you are now to where you want to be on the continuum.

Discussion with the Principal

Once you have a clear idea of your vision for the planning process, you will move to the second step—discussing your vision with the principal for her suggestions, support, and approval. Regardless of the change you decide on to help move you toward the circumstances and process described in Scenario 3, you should discuss it with the principal. A partner not only keeps the other partner informed but also relies on her for ideas, direction, and assistance.

Planning Team (Creation of a Library Media Advisory Committee)

The formation of a library media advisory committee (planning committee) composed of representatives of the learning community is the next step in the planning process and in broadening the base of support for and involvement in the library media program. This committee of representatives from the teaching, administrative, and support staff as well as parents, students, and the larger learning community will initiate the planning process. Although it is advisable to establish criteria to determine the membership of the library media advisory committee, consideration should be given to (1) the people identified in your "network of power and influence" developed in Chapter 1, which identified the people on whom you are most dependent, and (2) key staff and community members who will be most influential in the planning process as well as in the implementation of the plan. Having your principal be a member of this committee is key to its success. She must be a part of the process rather than learning about the plan when it is complete. You may consider including your main detractor as well. Being a part of the process may win this person over to the side of students and their needs. This committee does not have to function solely as the planning team for this project; it can also become a standing committee assisting you in all aspects of the library media program.

Planning Process

The next step is for the planning team to develop an action plan that will ensure the development of a planning process for the library media program composed of vision and mission statements as well as goals and objectives. Brainstorming and other idea-generating processes described in the previous chapter will be very helpful as the planning process proceeds.

Needs Assessment: Bridging the Gap between What Is and What Can Be

One of the first tasks in the action plan developed by the planning committee is to gather information on the current use of the library media center as well as on the services and programs desired in the future. Information gathering is the heart of the needs assessment process. The committee will identify the types of data to be collected concerning the present program and those that will be needed in the future, as well as develop and conduct the needs assessment. Both quantitative data (analyzing student performance as well as library media data such as collection, circulation, planning sessions) and qualitative data (surveys, interviews, observations, anecdotes, focus groups) should be collected to gain an accurate picture of the present program. Important sources of data include: present collection and usage; future interests of staff and students; student achievement including achievement of information literacy standards; research on library media programs that represent best practice and innovative programming; and local instructional programming as well as national trends that may impact the library media program. Additionally, school or district policies such as the media center staffing level, the media center budget (which impacts on both the collection and facility), and resource selection as well as other policies or lack of policies should be considered.

A needs survey can be readily created by using any of four powerful resources or a combination thereof: *Purdue Self-Evaluation System* [PSES] *for Media Centers* (Loertscher & Stroud, 1976); *Information Power: Building Partnerships for Learning* (AASL & AECT, 1998); *Program Evaluation: Library Media Services* (Fitzpatrick, 1998); and *A Planning Guide for Information Power: Building Partnerships for Learning with School Library Media Program Assessment Rubric for the 21st Century* (AASL, 1999). PSES is a catalog of statements that encompasses nine broad categories: accessibility, awareness, professionalism, utilization, planning, acquisition, production, evaluation, and activity. This catalog will assist you in tailoring a needs assessment for your specific program. *Information Power* provides a comprehensive overview of the library media program, including standards, principles, and goals from which needs assessment statements may be developed. *Program Evaluation* is a guide for standards-based program evaluation including Information Literacy Standards (AASL), a rubric for each standard, and methodology for evaluating student learning. (A rubric is a method of assessment that describes a continuum of levels of students' achievement of a standard.) This document, which is very comprehensive, will provide information from which to develop statements on student learning. Finally, *A Planning Guide for Information Power* provides a planning process for the development of a library media program together with a rubric encompassing the roles of the library media specialist: teaching and learning, information access and delivery, and program administration. This document gives excellent direction in developing a comprehensive needs assessment as well.

Several years ago, as part of their library media curriculum guide, the library media staff of a large city school district, using PSES, developed a "bank" of survey statements from which school-level library media specialists could draw to develop a needs survey specific for their library media program. Also included in this curriculum guide was a bank of goals and objectives developed by the library media staff and keyed to specific needs statements. When the survey responses were analyzed, the library media specialist could go to the bank of goals and objectives to select those that addressed the specific needs. A similar district-level bank of survey statements can be developed by using any of the resources or combination of resources described here. The bank of needs statements, as well as the bank of goals and objectives, provide valuable assistance for both the building-level media specialist and the library media committee. Examples of needs survey statements adapted from PSES are included at the end of this chapter.

The data from all assessment elements will help you determine how the library media center is presently being used, identify strengths and areas of need, and provide suggestions for services and programs that the learning community feels will strengthen the program in the future. An analysis of this data will identify the gap between what is and what should be. Leadership involves seeing this gap before others do, convincing them that there is indeed a gap, and then shepherding the process to ensure that the learning community moves beyond it.

Vision, Mission, Goals, and Objectives

Now that the needs have been defined, both the vision and mission statements for the library media program can be developed. Even if you have created these statements for your program in the past, or have spent time in preliminary thinking and reflection about them, if you are moving toward Scenario 3 and want a broader base of support for the program, it is the library media advisory committee that must create these statements now.

Vision Statement. The vision statement describes a picture of the future library media program and its impact on student achievement. It is an ideal of what can be. Key to the vision statement is the student and his or her ability to function successfully as an information-literate adult as well as a contributing member of society in the 21st century. The vision should reflect (1) the local and national trends that impact the library media program, as well as (2) how the gap that was determined in the needs assessment will be closed. Elements that were identified as areas of need should be emphasized as well. For the vision of the media program to be accepted, the people who will be impacted by it should be involved at some level in its creation.

Mission Statement. The mission statement, which is derived from the vision, describes the purpose of the library media program—why the program exists. In preparation for the meeting at which the mission statement will be developed, you may wish to share a copy of the mission statement found in *Information Power* (1998) with members of the committee. It is an excellent resource in creating both the vision and the mission statements.

Goals and Objectives. When the vision and mission statements have been developed, the library media advisory committee must develop specific goals and objectives to address needs identified in the gap. Goals describe the steps required to attain the vision, and objectives are steps that show how to achieve those goals. Again, using available resources such as PSES, *Information Power* (1998), *Program Evaluation: Library Media Services*, and *A Planning Guide for Information Power* (1999), the committee should develop goal and objective statements. It is very helpful if a bank of statements can be established at the district or system level, thereby reducing the amount of time individual media specialists and library media advisory committees spend on developing these tools.

Action Plan. An action plan derived from the objectives is then created by the library media advisory committee and includes a reasonable timeline for implementation of each action step.

Further Broadening the Base of Support

Although the library media advisory committee may have already articulated vision, mission, goals, and objectives, these statements may have been shared primarily with the principal. As you enlarge the base of support, these planning tools are shared with members of the learning community for their input and evaluation, advancing to the position where teachers, administrators, other staff members, and students feel ownership of the library media program and where collaboration takes place as a systematic part of program. Once the vision statement is complete, it can be distributed to teachers, administrators, other staff members, and a representative group of students, parents, and the larger learning community. This should be accompanied by a carefully constructed letter inviting their participation in responding to the vision statement, an explanation of the purpose of the process, and a description of the method of participation. The statement and letter can be distributed by members of the committee or placed in mailboxes.

One process that can be used very successfully to achieve participation in the process without convening a group is the *Delphi Method*. It can be done completely through the mail, including electronic mail. In the first step, participants receive a copy of the prepared vision statement and are asked to mark items they agree with as well as write in suggested modifications. In the second step, all responses are collected and collated. A report is written and distributed to all participants. This report identifies areas of agreement and indicates how many people approved of each statement or wrote very similar statements. Next, each participant is asked to review his or her previous answer for possible revision. Any new responses that are clearly opposite from the vision statement recommended by the majority are noted and questioned for reasons, which are reported to the other participants. Asking participants who have opposite responses from the majority to give their reasons causes those without strong beliefs to move toward the middle; those who feel they have good rationale for their opposing opinions are likely to maintain and advocate them. This process proceeds for two more rounds, repeating the previous round exactly as described, and regarding the result of the fourth round to be as close to consensus as is possible (Schmuck, Runkel, Arends, & Arends, 1977, 174–175). When the vision statement is complete, the library media committee duplicates the process for the mission statement and, finally, for the goals and objectives. Although this generally takes place over an extended period, it is a process that achieves the objective of having a broad base of involvement as well as creating a sense of ownership among the participants. Regardless of the extent of involvement each library media committee wishes to foster, the Delphi Method can be used successfully. Although few committees have full participation of the teaching staff, a significant number of staff members and others will be willing to participate because of the rapport you have already established with them.

As you move along the continuum in planning your library media program, broadening your base of support, the library media program will grow proportionately. Moreover, collaborative planning as well as the program's impact on student achievement will be evident.

When you reach the point at which the teaching staff helps to create the library media program, that staff will have ownership of the program and will work for its successful implementation.

Implementation and Evaluation

Now that the tools for planning have been designed, the next step is implementation. The tools provide direction for program on a daily as well as long-term basis and become the means of evaluating the library media program. However, only by working with this plan for a full school year will you know if it is realistic. If you find that some of the goals and objectives are unachievable, select those goals and objectives that you feel are achievable and work with these for the remainder of the year. The successful completion of some of the objectives is dependent on the participation of other members of the learning community. These members must assume some of the responsibility to ensure that the goals and objectives are met.

At the end of the school year, evaluate all goals and objectives to determine the level of accomplishment for each. This information should be shared with the principal in a conference and in your annual report. It should include not only the evaluation of each objective but also future strategies for accomplishing long-range goals. The effectiveness of the library media program should be evaluated on the extent of its contributions to the improvement of the instructional program, in addition to how well it meets the needs of teachers and students. This information should be shared with staff and other members of the learning community.

If, during the evaluation of the program, you find that specific objectives are not being attained, this needs to be reported as well. In addition, each objective that is not achieved must be analyzed to determine why it was not achieved. Here is an example of an objective that was not fully achieved: "Before the end of the school year, 50 percent of the teaching staff will plan collaboratively with the library media specialist to integrate information literacy standards into their curriculum, by creating at least one authentic learning experience for students." In considering the reasons why this objective was not achieved, there are numerous possibilities: the library media specialist did not have adequate time to plan with teachers; the library media center had few resources available in particular subject areas; teachers did not find the "right" time or "right" authentic learning experience on which to plan collaboratively; teachers did not have an understanding of information literacy standards; teachers did not have adequate time to plan with the library media specialist; teachers taught their subject area from a textbook rather than by using resources found in the library media center as well as outside the center. Solutions to these problems will generate many opportunities for professional development that can be conducted by the principal, the library media specialist, teachers within the school, and experts in the field. These solutions also provide excellent justification for budget adjustments and may generate additional funds for resources, equipment, space, and/or staff.

Two outstanding resources are available for the evaluation of the library media program: *A Planning Guide for Information Power: Building Partnerships for Learning with School Library Media Program Assessment Rubric for the 21st Century* (AASL, 1999) and *Program Evaluation: Library Media Services* (Fitzpatrick, 1998). The *School Library Media Program*

Assessment Rubric for the 21st Century is designed as a self-assessment tool by which the library media specialist and building administrator, working together, assess the media program with the goal of improving it. The identification of different levels of program quality greatly improves the possibility that this goal will be achieved. *Program Evaluation: Library Media Services* includes a rubric for each of the "Information Literacy Standards for Student Learning" found in *Information Power: Building Partnerships for Learning* (AASL & AECT, 1998, 9–43). *Program Evaluation: Library Media Services* provides a framework for program evaluation while focusing on the quality of student work.

SOME FINAL WORDS

The library media program that will help students become information literate and able to function in the 21st century must be planned in collaboration with and "belong to" members of the learning community. An annual assessment of what is most important to members of the learning community should be conducted by the library media specialist and the library media committee. After analyzing the results of the assessment, the library media specialist, in collaboration with the library media advisory committee, will select those goals and objectives that address specific needs, prioritize these, and share them with members of the learning community; develop an action plan for each of the objectives; implement the plan; conduct an evaluation at the end of the school year to determine to what degree the goals and objectives were achieved; and share this information with administrators, teachers, and other staff. The program should be regularly monitored and adjusted throughout the year. A needs assessment should be administered again at the beginning of the next school year, and the process begun anew. This is a dynamic process that is never completed. Every several years, the library media committee should revisit the vision and adjust it, as well as the goals and objectives, to respond to new information. The mission will most likely remain constant.

AN EXEMPLARY SCHOOL LIBRARY MEDIA PROGRAM

Planning the library media program through use of these working tools at both the district and school levels is the method used in the following scenario from the Gwinnett County Public School System, a large suburban school district in Lawrenceville, Georgia, near Atlanta.

Gwinnett County Public School System, serving approximately 100,000 students in 81 schools, employs 100 library media specialists and 4 district coordinators. In the State of Georgia, each district and school is required to have a site-based decisionmaking team, an instructional technology plan, and a local school plan for improvement. In addition, since 1973 all elementary schools are required to be flexibly scheduled; and in 1978 all schools were requested to form a school media committee. This committee is responsible for program planning—the selection of goals and objectives; the selection of resources; the appeal process for library media materials; and recommendations concerning fund expenditures. An administrator, instructional staff members, and parents make up this committee, which is chaired by the library media specialist.

Anne Craft, the coordinator of media and instructional technology for the Gwinnett County Public Schools, Lawrenceville, Georgia, describes how these planning tools were developed in the Gwinnett Schools:

In 1981, each school was asked to complete a survey describing both the current state of the library media program as well as the desired state where each school wished their library media program to be in five years. The schools used the Purdue Self-Evaluation System (PSES) to assess their program. With the information submitted from schools, a group of library media specialists and myself analyzed the results, reviewed areas of strength as well as areas of need, developed a vision for where the district library media program should be in five years, and created a plan that included program purposes or goals for the library media program to achieve that vision. The goals, which remain the same as those developed at that time, follow: "To provide media resources, facilities, services and staff to support all areas of the instructional program; To provide a variety of services for students which develop skills and encourage the pursuit of lifelong learning; To develop procedures which allow optimum accessibility and effective utilization of all resources and the flexibility necessary to individualize instruction for students." Although the goals are the same, the objectives have changed and continue to change regularly as circumstances shift, thus helping library media specialists attain their goals. The objectives are created by each School Media Committee.

In 1993, library media specialists created a mission statement for the library media program with input from the total staff. The mission statement follows: "The mission of Media and Instructional Technology is to provide quality media, technology, and information services in order to enhance learning and ensure access to ideas and information for all."

In 1994–1995, local school technology coordinators and library media specialists worked with teachers, building principals, central office administrators, and community representatives to develop an Instructional Technology Plan that included a vision for instructional technology. This vision as well as the district vision shapes the vision of the Media and Instructional Technology program: "Gwinnett County Public Schools will be a system of world-class schools where students acquire the knowledge and skills to be successful as they continue their education at the postsecondary level and/or enter the work force." (Anne Craft, personal communication, March 18, 1999)

Deborah Klug is library media specialist at the J. P. McConnell Middle School (a suburban school of 1,200 students and one of the Gwinnett County Public Schools) in Loganville, Georgia. Deborah explains how program goals are developed:

As part of the district procedure, McConnell's Local School Plan for Improvement (LSPI), which includes goals that address specific needs, is drafted annually by the administrators and then reviewed by staff and members of the learning community. The academic focus of the LSPI is on the areas of reading, mathematics, and writing. Each teacher is annually responsible for selecting two goals—an instructional goal, which addresses student learning in one of the areas stipulated in the annual LSPI, as well as a professional development goal.

In addition to the Media and Instructional Technology department goals and the LSPI school goals, the School Media Committee, which I chair, develops goals for the library media center that are derived from the LSPI goals. The library goals, in a given year, may concentrate on building the professional collection to support instructional strategies, focus on particular aspects of research skills development, and develop programs that support not only recreational reading but also the skills necessary for content area reading.

Actual objectives for accomplishing the schoolwide goals are developed and implemented by teachers through a process called the Results Based Evaluation System (RBES.) Because I currently head the reading initiative in the school, I assist numerous teachers in developing an instructional or professional goal that addresses reading. Based on the idea of direct assistance rather than evaluation, teachers invite me to their classrooms to observe a lesson that is indicative of the implementation plan they set to achieve their reading goal. Finally, in April, we meet in post-observation conferences where we can discuss ways teachers implemented their goals and look at refinement for future years. I function as a teacher leader in this role. (Deborah Klug, personal communication, February 10, 1999)

The Gwinnett County Public School System is highly successful in planning the vision, mission, and goals at the district level with broadly based involvement of the learning community. Library media specialists lead the development not only of media program goals but also of instructional goals and objectives at the school level, that move the library media program as well as the instructional program toward achievement of the vision.

WHAT CAN I DO TO IMPLEMENT A PROGRAM PLANNING PROCESS FOR THE LIBRARY MEDIA PROGRAM?

- Establish a working relationship with members of the learning community based on mutual respect, fairness, honesty, flexibility, and trust.

- Read *Information Power: Building Partnerships for Learning* (AASL & AECT, 1998), and embrace the concepts of vision, mission, goals, objectives, principles, leadership, and collaboration.

- Commit yourself to planning your program by using these components. Exercise your leadership skills, and conceptualize the project. Answer the questions, "Why is this important to my library media program? to the instructional program?" Be prepared to explain its importance within the instructional program.

- Begin slowly by gathering supporters, and continue to enlarge the base of support by collaborating on these planning components with a library media advisory committee and then with members of the learning community.

- With the principal, complete a comprehensive assessment of your program by using the *School Library Media Program Assessment Rubric for the 21st Century*, found in *A Planning Guide for Information Power: Building Partnerships for Learning* (AASL, 1999), and create a plan to improve your library media program.

EXAMPLE OF NEEDS SURVEY STATEMENTS

(Adapted from PSES with permission
from David Loertscher)

PLEASE USE THE FOLLOWING SCALE FOR ASSESSMENT OF BOTH THE
CURRENT SITUATION AS WELL AS THE DESIRED LEVEL.

1 Regularly
2 Occasionally
3 Rarely/Never
4 Don't Know
5 Does Not Apply

INSTRUCTION	CURRENT	DESIRED
1. The library media staff delivers a program of		
reading guidance.	1 2 3 4 5	1 2 3 4 5
viewing and listening guidance.	1 2 3 4 5	1 2 3 4 5
research guidance.	1 2 3 4 5	1 2 3 4 5
integration of information skills into content.	1 2 3 4 5	1 2 3 4 5
integration of information literacy standards.	1 2 3 4 5	1 2 3 4 5

COMMENT(S) ————————————————————————

	CURRENT	DESIRED
2. Information access skills are		
taught as a unit of instruction.	1 2 3 4 5	1 2 3 4 5
integrated into instructional units.	1 2 3 4 5	1 2 3 4 5
given informally upon request.	1 2 3 4 5	1 2 3 4 5

COMMENT(S)————————————————————————

	CURRENT	DESIRED
3. Staff development topics for teachers include		
integrating media center resources into instruction.	1 2 3 4 5	1 2 3 4 5
utilizing technology resources including e-mail and the Internet.	1 2 3 4 5	1 2 3 4 5
utilizing technology equipment.	1 2 3 4 5	1 2 3 4 5
existing media center services.	1 2 3 4 5	1 2 3 4 5
new additions to media center services.	1 2 3 4 5	1 2 3 4 5

COMMENT(S)————————————————————————

4. Library media staff assist teachers in unit
    planning by   CURRENT   DESIRED
          gathering resources.   1 2 3 4 5   1 2 3 4 5
          preparing bibliographies.   1 2 3 4 5   1 2 3 4 5
          consulting in advance of unit
              presentation.   1 2 3 4 5   1 2 3 4 5
          suggesting resources for unit.   1 2 3 4 5   1 2 3 4 5
          assisting in analysis of learning tasks. 1 2 3 4 5   1 2 3 4 5
          collaborating on unit development,
              implementation, and assessment.   1 2 3 4 5   1 2 3 4 5
    COMMENT(S)_____

5. Collaboratively, teachers and media center
    staff assess the success of
          class projects involving the library
              media center.   1 2 3 4 5   1 2 3 4 5
          small-group projects involving the
              library media center.   1 2 3 4 5   1 2 3 4 5
          individual projects involving the
              library media center.   1 2 3 4 5   1 2 3 4 5
          integration of information skills.   1 2 3 4 5   1 2 3 4 5
          integration of information literacy
              standards.   1 2 3 4 5   1 2 3 4 5
          jointly planned units of instruction.   1 2 3 4 5   1 2 3 4 5
    COMMENT(S)_____

6. Teachers have adequate time to plan with
    the library media staff.   1 2 3 4 5   1 2 3 4 5

7. Teachers are given information about
          new resources in the library media
              center.   1 2 3 4 5   1 2 3 4 5
          new equipment in the library media
              center.   1 2 3 4 5   1 2 3 4 5
          services available through interlibrary
              loan.   1 2 3 4 5   1 2 3 4 5
          community resources (guests, field
              trips, etc.).   1 2 3 4 5   1 2 3 4 5
          existing media center services.   1 2 3 4 5   1 2 3 4 5
          information literacy standards for
              student learning.   1 2 3 4 5   1 2 3 4 5
    COMMENT(S)_____

8. The library media staff provides teachers
    with opportunities to evaluate   CURRENT   DESIRED

	CURRENT	DESIRED
library media collection.	1 2 3 4 5	1 2 3 4 5
library media services.	1 2 3 4 5	1 2 3 4 5
library media facilities.	1 2 3 4 5	1 2 3 4 5
library media policies.	1 2 3 4 5	1 2 3 4 5

COMMENT(S)_____

FACILITY/COLLECTION

9. The library media center is used for

class use on teacher request.	1 2 3 4 5	1 2 3 4 5
small groups on teacher request.	1 2 3 4 5	1 2 3 4 5
individual student research.	1 2 3 4 5	1 2 3 4 5
individual student enjoyment.	1 2 3 4 5	1 2 3 4 5
regularly scheduled classes.	1 2 3 4 5	1 2 3 4 5
other _____	1 2 3 4 5	1 2 3 4 5

COMMENT(S)_____

---

10. The media center collection, in general,

is up-to-date.	1 2 3 4 5	1 2 3 4 5
is visually appealing.	1 2 3 4 5	1 2 3 4 5
supports the curriculum.	1 2 3 4 5	1 2 3 4 5
represents a broad range of student interests and needs.	1 2 3 4 5	1 2 3 4 5
represents a broad range of staff interests and needs.	1 2 3 4 5	1 2 3 4 5
represents all sides of controversial issues.	1 2 3 4 5	1 2 3 4 5
is void of racial, ethnic, or sexual bias.	1 2 3 4 5	1 2 3 4 5

COMMENT(S)_____

Collaborative Planning: Redefining a Partnership with Teachers

5

Because the focus of education is on student achievement, we as library media specialists must demonstrate how the library media program positively impacts student learning. In order to do so, we must become a full partner with the classroom teacher in the planning, implementation, and assessment of the curriculum –the instructional program. As the library media program is restructured, the instructional program will be restructured as well. A partnership among the principal, classroom teachers, and you, the library media specialist, is a requirement if this restructuring of education is to become a reality. Collaborative planning is the vehicle by which to construct this partnership, and resource-based learning is the process by which to restructure the instructional program for students. Library media specialists are in a unique position to facilitate this restructuring as they collaborate as a curriculum partner with classroom teachers, one person or one team at a time.

WHAT IS THE CURRICULUM ROLE OF THE LIBRARY MEDIA SPECIALIST?

Curriculum is the center of the instructional program, and the library media program is the underpinning of the curriculum. For us as library media specialists to function as full curriculum partners with classroom teachers, we must use our leadership skills to become knowledgeable about their curriculum, understand curriculum design, and participate in its creation; create a library information skills curriculum; develop the collection in collaboration with teachers and staff to meet the instructional needs of the school; collaborate with classroom teachers on the planning, implementation, and assessment of the instructional program; link student needs, information literacy standards as well as information skills, and resources across all curricular areas through meaningfully integrated curricular units; effectively teach information skills and a research process through these units; understand as well as participate in the assessment of student learning; and be passionate about our work as well as dedicated to the improvement of the teaching and learning process.

As a foundation, we, as the practitioners of this profession and aspiring curriculum partners, must have an information skills curriculum that uses state or national learning standards as a framework and emphasizes process rather than content. For example, the emphasis should be on the processes students use in the successful completion of a student project rather than on how to use a specific resource. This guide should also include benchmarks that will help evaluate student learning. If this curriculum is not presently available in your district, it must be developed in collaboration with other library media specialists in the district or region. Many school districts have already created this document using local or national standards as their framework. Check with library media specialists in nearby school districts. Guides can also be found in professional literature and on the World Wide Web. Use any of these sources to get you started. As an example, visit the Internet for the "Mankato Schools Information Literacy Curriculum Guidelines," Mankato, Minnesota, at: <http://www.isd77.k12.mn.us/resources/infocurr/infolit.html> and the "Makato (MN) Grade Level Benchmarks for Media and Technology", Mankato, Minnesota, at: <http://www.isd77.k12.mn.us/resources/infocurr/benchmark.html>.

As a curriculum partner, we want to demonstrate that information literacy standards and skills are an integral part of the curriculum. This is generally introduced during the planing step of an instructional unit. However, if these elements are written into the curriculum at the time of its development at the departmental or district level, then when you and the classroom teacher begin planning a unit, the teacher will accept these elements as part of his or her curriculum. Library media specialists must become members of curriculum committees at the departmental or district level as all curriculum is being written. Although this may be daunting, especially in a small district, it is an important goal. It will greatly assist you as you plan with each teacher. Entering the curriculum process at its inception affords the greatest opportunity to become a curriculum partner.

Gayle Collins, part-time district technology coordinator for the Northfield Public Schools, a small suburban district in Northfield, Minnesota, and part-time library media specialist at Northfield High School (with an enrollment of 1,500 students), also feels that work in curriculum development is central to her role. She believes that the library media specialist must enter the curricular process at the foundational level and build the curriculum with subject area teachers:

Information literacy standards must be integrated into the curriculum at the initial stage of the planning process. This is the only way we are able to successfully integrate information skills into the curriculum. I have found that whenever I have had to go back and infuse the information skills into a unit after the curriculum is written, it is always viewed by the teacher as an add-on that is not taken seriously and viewed as less important than the unit itself. In school districts that have a regular cycle of curriculum revision, the participation in the process for each department or grade level will be easier and more satisfying for both you and the classroom or subject area teachers. As teachers write new or evaluate existing units, we are a partner in the process. When the teacher is ready to implement the unit, our partnership is a normal part of the unit. (Gayle Collins, personal communication, May 17, 1999)

In this chapter, as well as in Chapter 6, specific processes, techniques, and strategies are discussed that will enable you to function at each step of instructional design and to achieve the role of curriculum partner.

COLLABORATIVE PLANNING

If library media specialists are to participate in instructional design and be a curriculum partner, we must begin at the first step—planning. Research and practice demonstrate that traditional teacher library/media specialist planning has not been completely successful. In addition, research also reveals that the perception many classroom teachers have of our role differs from our perception of our role. It is important that we identify a planning process that provides more consistent results as we plan with teachers, change teachers' perceptions of our role, learn the skills of collaborative planning, and have the ability and knowledge to introduce resource-based learning in the planning and implementation of curricular projects and units. At the same time, information literacy standards must be integrated into the instructional program.

A Historical Perspective

During the past forty years, as educators responded to research and practice, they began to see the value of integrating the library media program into the instructional program. Research indicated that teaching skills in isolation was not productive to student learning. Greater attention was directed at the learning process rather than at the outcomes. With a movement away from a single textbook and lecture methodology to student involvement in his or her learning, library media specialists subscribed to the concept of resource-based teaching and learning, which exemplified this changing philosophy and was facilitated through the library media program. Cooperative program planning or teacher/library media specialist planning was the terminology used to explain this curriculum phenomenon. Although much attention was directed at describing and encouraging this relationship, little attention was directed at the nature of this relationship or the process of curriculum planning (Doiron, 1993, 11).

In cooperative planning, classroom teachers came to the planning process prepared to share knowledge of their student needs and curriculum content. Library media specialists came to the process with their expertise in resources and information skills. In this linear type of planning, both individuals planned separately and then examined their programs to determine common objectives that could be developed from the resources available in the library media center (Doiron, 1993, 12).

Even though both parties usually felt positive about the experience, sometimes conflict arose between them. The classroom teacher often entered the planning process at the activity level whereas the library media specialist entered at the goal-setting level. Although classroom teachers may have understood the behavioristic or linear planning model, many had created a more informal style in which they felt more comfortable. While many library media specialists reported that their first efforts to cooperatively plan with classroom teachers were successful, they also reported that teachers were often unwilling to participate in subsequent units or projects (Doiron, 1993, 12, 13).

Although the professional literature has described curriculum involvement of the library media specialist for many years, research over time has concluded that with few exceptions library media specialists have not been involved in instructional planning at any consistent level (Wolcott, 1994, 161).

Perceptions of the Role of the Library Media Specialist

Further complicating the participation of the library media specialist in the planning process is the perception that many teachers have of our role. In a survey conducted in 1997, DeGroff (1997) found that teachers, like principals, believed that the library media specialist was practicing the information specialist and teacher roles but felt that the instructional consultant role—the participation of the library media specialist in developing, implementing, and assessing unit experiences—was less important. Teachers most valued the assistance library media specialists provided in selecting resources for unit experiences—the information specialist role (12, 18).

In another survey conducted by Pickard in 1991 on the instructional consultant role, whereas 90 percent of the library media specialists indicated that this role was important, less than half of these specialists were actually attempting to integrate this role in their program to any great extent. In a follow-up study, Pickard found that 62 percent of the library media specialists responding reported involvement in resource-based units at only the supporting level and not at the instructional consultant level. We can conclude that library media specialists only supplied resources for the teachers who created, implemented, and assessed the resource-based unit rather than participating in the process. Teachers continue to see us only in the support role that we have played in the past (Pickard, 1994, 27, 29).

Pickard (1994) shares some interesting observations by library media specialists. "Some teachers still feel you are trying to take over their role as teacher." "Some teachers are reluctant to 'invite' you into their domain." "Many teachers have little knowledge of library and research skills. Therefore, they are not comfortable working with the library media specialist." "Teacher education should pave the way. The library media specialist is never considered when the team teaching concept is taught" (28). Clearly there is work to be done.

Finally, research conducted by Wolcott, Lawless, and Hobbs (1999) with preservice teachers confirmed the earlier studies and concluded that learning and teaching as well as the program administration function were not well understood; that preservice teachers identified most with the library media specialist as a resource manager and information specialist; and that preservice teachers do not share the vision of the library media specialist as partner and leader in instruction (2).

What Can We Do to Change the Teachers' Perceptions?

Although it is possible that the perception classroom teachers hold about our role limits our participation in the curricular process, the perception we hold of ourselves can also limit our participation. Indeed, our perception is pivotal to how others view us. If we view our role as basically that of an information specialist and not of a teacher or curriculum partner, teachers will embrace the "keeper of the books" stereotype. If we are proactive and demonstrate the benefits of an integrated library media program with enthusiasm, expertise, confidence, and flexibility, showing how these will assist teachers in teaching their content area more successfully while improving student learning, we will change teachers' perceptions. We must understand the curriculum partner role and demonstrate our curricular expertise, which is derived from our knowledge of resources and their applications within the curriculum addressing the needs of students. Collectively we, the practitioners of this profession, must agree on our role—teacher, instructional partner, information specialist, and program administrator—and move rapidly to change perceptions by speaking with a unified voice so that everyone understands our role and can expect other library media specialists to function in the same manner.

Develop an Understanding of the Teachers' Role

Classroom teachers experience the same type of challenges that we do. Instead of complaining about the lack of understanding from your teachers, we should gain a better appreciation for the breadth of their daily responsibilities and provide them with service at the level where they are presently functioning: at their point of need.

Teachers work with a classroom or multiple classrooms of individual students who have specific needs and wants; they make hundreds of decisions each day, often with little or no opportunity to reflect; they carry on many operations concurrently; they deal with constant interruptions within their classrooms as well as from outside; they feel isolated from other adults; they are continually adapting to change; they constantly feel a lack of time to complete their daily tasks or to reflect on the bigger picture of what they do and, as a result, become focused on the day-to-day, short-term operations of their classroom; and they rely more on their experiential knowledge than on sources of knowledge outside their classrooms such as professional literature and staff development (Fullan, 1991, 33, 34). They are very busy people with a finite amount of time to teach and improve their instructional programs.

Having an understanding of the demands placed daily on teachers and being sensitive to their frustrations, helping them understand how you can relieve some of their burden, will enable you to better work together. Supporting teachers in this way is the first step in developing a partnership.

Even though your position may include as many complex variables as the teachers' you must find or reallocate time and energy to develop partnerships with them. Implementation of the following suggestions will begin to change perceptions.

- Share ideas with teachers or provide informal staff development; these are important steps in the creation of rapport as well as a validation of your competence.

- Be proactive—do not wait for teachers to come to you. Extend yourself through a variety of approaches including personal interactions and written communications. Target a group of teachers, a team, a grade level on which to concentrate the program. Provide information and resources for both their professional and their personal interests.

- Develop an understanding about how critical it is that students become information literate and why these standards should be integrated into the context of their instructional program.

- Broaden your base of support. Join school committees and afterschool activities. Let people see you outside of the library media center.

- Describe an idea or offer a service more than once. It can take up to thirty-five repetitions for learning to take place (Haycock, 1991a, 62).

In a workshop setting with Philip Turner (1996), teachers shared ideas on ways in which library media specialists could assist them with their instructional programs. The group prioritized services in three levels. In the highest level, the in-depth level, teachers suggested that library media specialists provide staff development on the newest multimedia resources, the latest instructional techniques, and motivational strategies; and work with teachers to plan curriculum lessons. At the moderate level, teachers suggested that media specialists locate resources, provide information and assistance in areas such as conflict resolution, and provide assistance in developing effective instructional strategies as well as in implementing instructional activities. At the initial level, they suggested that library media specialists provide sample lesson plans on a broad range of topics, share information about new resources in the media center, and provide the most current instructional resources available (209). Although this information cannot be generalized to all teachers, these are excellent suggestions to offer teachers as examples of services that we can provide. As we persevere in following these avenues that promote support, we will change perceptions while building partnerships with classroom teachers.

Learn How to Plan Collaboratively

Much of traditional planning is considered cooperative or parallel planning, in which both the teacher and library media specialist begin the planning process separately, then combine their individual results, and finally try to merge the goals and content of both programs (Doiron, 1993, 12). This type of planning has often been problematic. In contrast, collaborative planning is a philosophical framework, a method of thinking about teaching and learning, a process by which to improve the instructional program, and a strategy for working more successfully with classroom teachers and students (Haycock, 1991b).

Following is a step-by-step strategy for collaborative planning with the classroom teacher.

- Work with the principal to establish a common planning time, perhaps once every four to six weeks. Both you and the classroom teachers must have the time to plan. If planning is a part of the teacher's responsibility, it will become a normal activity. If it is something the principal does not view as critical to the instructional process, teachers may feel the same way.

- Make contact with a teacher with whom you have planned curricular units in the past, and establish a time to discuss an upcoming unit. If you are an elementary library media specialist, it is important that your library media center be flexibly scheduled so that you are available to plan with teachers. Chapter 3 of this book gives a step-by-step procedure for implementing flexible scheduling. If possible, learn the topic of the project or unit before the planning session, and be prepared with some resources to share when the teacher arrives.

- Discuss and reflect with the classroom teacher on the teaching and learning process. Encourage this teacher to share his rich experiences and information about students, curriculum, and methodology. Through discussion, your common concerns and experiences will be identified, and both you and the classroom teacher will gain an understanding, appreciation, and acceptance for the other partner as well as for your interrelated roles (Doiron, 1993, 14; Wolcott, 1994, 163). Although this exchange is time consuming at the outset, the process will proceed more quickly thereafter. You will also not collaborate on every assignment on which students work in the library media center.

- Understand teachers' planning styles. Teachers plan for a variety of reasons: to increase their sense of security; to be prepared with all aspects of a lesson—content, resources, and activities; and to fulfill the requirement to maintain and submit written plans regularly to the administrator. Much of the teacher's planning is done by thinking and reflecting about the lesson or unit; it is not written down on paper. Most often, the plans that are written down provide a mere outline or list of activities. Studies show that the linear planning model described earlier in this chapter does not represent the planning style of the experienced classroom teacher of today. Teachers today focus more on the content and activities and less on the objectives and evaluation. Finally, the textbook, published curriculum guides, and teachers' guides for the content studied and methodologies used greatly influence planning as well (Wolcott, 1994, 162, 163).

- Allow each teacher to take the lead in the planning process and determine which style you will follow. Regardless of where you begin the process, you will be able to include all the important elements: goals, content, methodology, activities, and assessment. Be prepared to accommodate several types and styles of planning. Remember that planning is often something we do by ourselves, a mental activity rather than a verbal exchange. Planning collaboratively may be difficult and even unwelcome on the part of the classroom teacher. It may also be difficult for you for the same reasons. Until the classroom teacher comes to expect to collaborate with you, it may be necessary to reinforce the reasons for planning and the attendant benefits to students.

- Determine early in the planning session what the teacher wishes to accomplish—what students will learn and be able to do at the end of the unit (Wiggins & McTighe, 1998, 9–13). Brainstorm and discuss ideas and strategies that will make the teacher feel comfortable with the process.

- Decide on a variety of acceptable assessments for the unit (Wiggins & McTighe, 1998, 9–13). These might include, but are not limited to, performance such as an oral or written report, debate, creation of a poem, construction of a model, demonstration, role-play, or use of electronic media. Develop a rubric, checklist, or other tools if these are appropriate for the project or unit. In addition to determining the method of assessment, be a partner in the assessment process. Assessment will be discussed more fully in Chapter 6.

- Plan the learning activities for students as well as the instruction (Wiggins & McTighe, 1998, 9–13). Frequently, it is at this activity level that most teachers wish to enter the planning process. These last three steps are described by Wiggins and McTighe (1998) as "The Backward Design" of curriculum planning.

- When planning the activities, develop essential questions about the topic. According to Wiggins and McTighe (1998), essential questions are those that teach for understanding, engage students in uncovering important ideas about the topic, and go to the heart of the subject. These questions have no right answers, generate more questions about the topic, and are designed to sustain students' interest in the topic (26–34).

- Link resources with the curriculum and the needs of students. Resources should include print, technology, and the Internet; they should be available within the school and beyond, including human resources.

- Always tailor the planning session to the needs and style of the individual teacher (Wolcott, 1994, 163, 164).

These steps in the planning process will help you collaboratively plan with the classroom teacher and ensure that you become a full curriculum partner in the instructional program.

Practices from Outstanding
Library Media Specialists and Teachers

Rhonda True, a sixth grade teacher and team leader at the Lux Middle School (a participant in the Library Power initiative with an enrollment of 950 students), Lincoln Public Schools, in Lincoln, Nebraska, relates:

Collaboration is the key to teaching information literacy and having students practice the skills through their curriculum in ways that are meaningful.

To promote collaboration, information literacy, and the teaching of a research path for students, our district developed a cadre of teachers and library media specialist that worked in partners to go into all schools in the district and model as well as share how collaboration can be done so that curricular objectives as well as information literacy standards are met.

Sixth grade is the entrance year for our students into a new building. We need to familiarize the students with our library media center as well as review "the Big6" [Eisenberg and Berkowitz, 1990] research path with them. Prior to beginning this unit, we meet with our library media specialist and plan resources and activities we want the students to use as well as what curricular objectives and information literacy standards we will integrate. Generally, we plan with the library media specialist during our plan time either individually or as a team. This unit is meant as an introduction, and the students spend only six days in the media center learning about the sources and then using them. We all share in the assessment of the projects. Now, as a team, we know students are familiar with the sources and the path to answering their questions.

Some teachers are resistant to collaborating. I think the best way to solve this problem is for the teachers who are hesitant to see other teachers collaborating and see the results for kids and teachers. Another great way is to do a team project and involve all teachers so they become a part of the process; usually after one time, the teacher recognizes that this is not an add-on but a way to integrate instructional objectives and have kids practice them in a relevant way. (Rhonda True, personal communication, January 23, 1999)

Becky Pasco, library media specialist at Lincoln High School (with an enrollment of 2,128 students and a participant in the Library Power initiative) Lincoln Public Schools, in Lincoln, Nebraska, reports:

I do individual conferencing to collaborate with my staff. It allows me to customize my services to the individual's needs and demeanor. I never try to work with teachers after school when they are tired—I want to catch them at times when they are physically and emotionally ready to learn (which is what research emphasizes we should do with all learners—adult or children). I invite them to breakfast or lunch, depending on their plan period, on a day they tell me they are available. I keep all collaboration to no more than 30 to 45 minutes of brainstorming, detail work, and discussion. Then we eat and socialize.

Part of any good collaboration effort is the public relations it extends. Even if I have not convinced a teacher at that point to bring his or her students to the library media center, I have made a new friend or reaffirmed an old friendship that will, most often, turn into a resource-based project in the future. Library media specialists often forget that they should have two groups in mind when collaborating: (1) increasing the information literacies of students through resource-based learning, and (2) increasing the information literacies of teachers. Many teachers grew up with library programs that were not proactive, so their own information literacies are weak. I also try to remember, when collaborating with teachers, to make sure the teachers leave our meeting feeling good about themselves as learners and educators. When this happens, I stand a better chance that they will eventually bring in their students to have the same good experience that they had. (Becky Pasco, personal communication, January 2, 1999)

Marjorie Rohrbach, one of the library media specialists at the Fuquay-Varina High School (a grade 9–12 high school with approximately 1,500 students), a participant in the Library Power initiative, in Wake County Public Schools in Raleigh, North Carolina, summarizes the collaborative process:

Collaborative planning did not take place with the wave of a magic wand. Just as one weeds a collection one item at a time, one often enlists the support of a staff one teacher at a time. In a collaborative atmosphere, all parties must check egos at the door; not always easy for professionals used to thinking "my program, my class, my lesson." We also need to recognize that not all information gathering requires elaborate collaboration. Sometimes students need to gather facts from very traditional resources. It is impractical and self-defeating to try to manufacture collaboration out of a "we need to look up state populations to plot a chart" reference experience. It is important to time your suggestions to their optimum use, and then teachers will also start to realize when they have an idea that is appropriate to a collaboratively planned research experience. Of course, it is ideal when the state population gathering class returns to compare, contrast, and analyze characteristics of world populations for an activity collaboratively planned by you and the classroom teacher.

One approach that I thought most successful in luring teachers to try collaboration is "The Box." This idea actually came directly from a Library Power–sponsored workshop. Barbara Stripling, Library Power director, then in Chattanooga, Tennessee, and coauthor of *Brainstorms and Blueprints: Teaching Library Research as a Thinking Process* (1988), offered the workshop, "Thoughtful Learning." One of the strategies offered for planning secondary research experiences was REACTS: A Taxonomy of Research Reactions. This tool identified higher-order thinking levels and corresponding activity and format suggestions. Barbara had color-coded the activities on index cards and filed them in a standard file box. I reproduced this product at my school and introduced it to a receptive English teacher as we planned some research for her classes. She borrowed "The Box" and took it to her planning room. The next thing I knew the entire English department wanted to know how to get one of those boxes. These cards continually provide us with an opening dialogue as we convince more staff members that collaborative planning is the most effective way for students to have a successful research experience with a meaningful end product. (Marjorie Rohrbach, personal communication, February 18, 1999). "The Box" will be described more fully in Chapter 6.

Sharon Vansickle, library media specialist and technology coordinator Norcross High School in the Gwinnett County School District, Lawrenceville, Georgia, relates an idea that has promoted collaborative planning with reluctant teachers:

We were conscious of the fact that when some students entered the library media center they were drawn to the technology. They had little direction when using the media center to do research. We decided to send a note to all teachers telling them that if they planned with one of the media specialists one week prior to the project, we would be able to help them and their students immensely by creating what we call "Pathfinders." These provide the teacher and student with a listing of potential database resources, books, and Internet sites that may be helpful in moving forward in the information search process. This has been a very successful way to encourage teachers to plan research projects with us. In some cases, it has led to more collaborative planning as well. (Sharon Vansickle, personal communication, May 10, 1999)

David Sanger, library media specialist at Baker Middle School (grades 6–8 with an enrollment of approximately 600 students), a participant in the Library Power initiative, in Denver, Colorado, reports:

When we became a Library Power School, there were three criteria with which we had to comply. First, we had to be flexibly scheduled, a requirement we already met. Second, we had to collaborate with teachers on the instructional program, which we needed to work on; and third, we were required to form a Library Power Leadership Team comprised of the principal, teachers, and library media specialist. We added a student and parent to this important catalyst for change in our library media program.

When we began the Library Power initiative, I interpreted the need to collaborate with teachers to mean "every" teacher in the school. Some were more receptive than others, but there were some who, regardless of my strategy, remained unwilling. As I wrestled with this dilemma and rethought my overall goal for program, I realized that it was the student who was the target of the library media program. While teachers' participation in the goal is critical, I could look at the participation of teams and ensure through collaboration with some teachers on every team that all students would participate in collaboratively planned units. At this time, every student is involved in at least two curricular units each year in which I collaborate with a teacher or team to plan the unit and help in its implementation as well as in its assessment. (David Sanger, personal communication, June 11, 1999)

The experiences related by these practitioners describe the challenges, opportunities, and accomplishments of collaborating with teachers in the instructional program to become a curriculum partner. Their techniques provide sound and rational counsel on how to proceed.

RESOURCE-BASED LEARNING

Understanding both how to collaboratively plan and its benefits to student learning, we now need to concentrate on an instructional process that will involve students in their learning. Resource-based learning will accomplish this. Resource-based *learning* is a process whereby students use a variety of resources to complete units of study; it places them at the center of their learning environment. Resource-based learning addresses the diversity of student abilities, multiple intelligences, and individual styles of learning (*Partners in Action*, 1982, 6–9). The focus of resource-based learning is students and how they use resources to facilitate their learning (Haycock, 1991c, 16).

Resource-based learning requires that the learning process and environment as well as the relationship between the teacher and student be restructured to facilitate student learning. The classroom teacher and library media specialist must design curricular units and structure the activities, as well as the location of the activities, to ensure that students will construct new knowledge by learning the big ideas through essential questions which will connect students with their instructional needs and resources in meaningful ways. As partners, the classroom teacher and library media specialist teach a research process and are facilitators of learning, providing feedback as well as guiding, questioning, and coaching students throughout the inquiry process to ensure their success. As a result, students "learn how to learn" by accessing, evaluating, and using a wide range of information from a variety of sources to achieve instructional objectives. They are engaged learners in their education in the classroom, library media center, and community, interacting with other students in a variety of group activities such as cooperative learning, discussion, role play, and debate. Through these activities they gain satisfaction from their accomplishments as well as self-confidence and independence. Also, they create a final product and presentation that demonstrates their understanding of and competence in the subject matter, and they are involved in the assessment of both the process and the product. Through the process, students become self-motivated and self-directed problem solvers as well as decisionmakers, acquiring important skills that they will use throughout their lives. Both members of this partnership (teacher and library media specialist) are involved in the assessment of the student's final product as well as the ongoing assessment of all aspects of the process (Haycock, 1991c, 16–19; *Partners in Action*, 1982, 6–9).

Although many of us have participated to some extent in resource-based learning as well as resource-based teaching (when classroom teachers use a variety of resources to supplement the textbook and when they are at the center of the learning environment), the regular use of resource-based learning projects and units calls for a restructuring of the instructional program. The units are collaboratively planned with the classroom teacher and the student is at the center of his or her learning environment, engaged in inquiry, and part of the assessment of both the process and the product.

Resources

A strong library media collection that has been developed by the library media specialist in collaboration with classroom teachers is necessary for resource-based learning. Students require a wide variety of resources available in a multitude of locations. These include, but are not limited to, the following: books, newspapers, periodicals, textbooks, maps, videos, videodiscs, CD-ROMs, computer hardware and software, online databases, and the Internet. Other resources can be found in the home, community, and beyond (e.g., museums, zoos, public and academic libraries, and businesses). Human resources are also important. These include individuals within the school (e.g., the library media specialist, teachers, administrators, and support staff) as well as people outside the school (e.g., parents and resource people from the community who are experts in their field such as communication, law, sports, business, and education). Although no collection can have all the resources necessary for resource-based learning, the world becomes a virtual library through accessing the Internet and using interlibrary loan.

Kim Carter, director of information and technology for Souhegan High School (with 950 students) in Amherst, New Hampshire, states:

For students to be actively involved in their learning, they must be directly, integrally, and meaningfully involved with information resources. One very significant impact is the need for as many primary source materials as possible. Because so much of the research is student-driven, I need to provide for a very broad range of research possibilities. And while it is broad, it also requires depth. I find there is a greater demand for very current information as well. As our curriculum develops, needs shift as do research areas. I need to constantly be looking for and thinking about how to maximize access to the widest possible range of information sources—that are user friendly. I've come to rely increasingly on online subscription services and to cultivate some reliable sources for information such as SCOUT REPORT, BLUEWEB'N, and BRITANNICA.COM. (Kim Carter, personal communication, June 8, 1999)

Charlotte Vlasis, library media specialist at the Chattanooga School for the Liberal Arts in Chattanooga, Tennessee, explains:

This grade K–8 school does not rely on textbooks as resources but on resource-based teaching and learning where the library media collection is rich in resources supporting many "hands-on" activities and projects. As a library media specialist, I am viewed as a resource person, a teacher, and a curriculum coordinator as well as partner. (Charlotte Vlasis, personal communication, June 2, 1999)

COLLABORATIVE PLANNING
AND RESOURCE-BASED LEARNING

In a research study conducted by Angela Isom in 1991 entitled "Collaborative Planning: The Teacher's and Administrator's Perspective" and described by Patricia W. Pickard (1994, 29), Isom found that whereas the large majority of both high school administrators and subject area teachers felt they were collaborative with the library media specialist, few truly collaborated with the media specialist in designing learning activities or units. Isom learned that even fewer felt that the involvement of the library media specialist would make any difference in the outcome of the instructional program. She concluded that "Possibly a faster and more significant change in practice and attitude, especially on the part of the teachers, will depend on an orchestrated effort ideally led by administrators rather than the one-on-one approach currently adopted and solely led by library media specialists" (Pickard, 1994, 29).

This research underscores the need to develop a partnership among the administrator, the classroom teacher, and yourself as library media specialist. These partnerships require complex change. Collaborative planning and resource-based learning require teachers to change not only the way they presently teach—using a textbook—but also the way they work with students—no longer autonomous but sharing both students and the responsibility with another person, the library media specialist. Collaborative planning and resource-based learning require the principal to provide strong leadership by demonstrating commitment. The administrator must (1) understand that these initiatives or restructuring of the library media program are actually a restructuring of the instructional program, and (2) believe that the restructured library media program will have a significant impact on student learning. While arranging for staff development and adequate time to plan for both teachers and the library media specialist, the administrator must give support to these other two members of the partnership (Meyer & Newton 1992, 18). (For a step-by-step planning model, refer to the section entitled Learn How to Plan Collaboratively earlier in this chapter.)

Resource-Based Learning Activities: Information Literacy for High School Students, by Anne Bleakley and Jackie L. Carrigan (1994), is a valuable addition to the library media specialist's professional collection. This book describes successful activity plans for a variety of subject areas. *Achieving a Curriculum-Based Library Media Center Program: The Middle School Model for Change*, by Jane Bandy Smith (1995), makes a distinction between resource-based and curriculum-based learning. It is another excellent resource.

Barbara Stein, library media specialist at Irving B. Weber Elementary School, Iowa City Community School District in Iowa City, Iowa, conducts a resource-based, collaboratively planned library media program utilizing a modified flexibly scheduled program for 425 students in a grades K–6 school. Resource-based teaching and learning is the foundation of the reading, social studies, and science programs throughout the district. There are no textbooks in these areas of the curriculum. Through the collaboration with classroom teachers on the development of curriculum, Barbara ensures that resources necessary to implement the unit are identified, the learning environment is created, and the facilitation and assessment of student learning are addressed. She also ensures that information literacy standards are integrated into the curriculum at the beginning of the planning process. She feels that partnering with teachers on the collaboration of program as well as the development of a resource-based teaching and learning program is a most important part of her role. Barbara describes the partnership and program:

When we create curricular units, we build in information literacy so that when the units are taught, the process is seamless—the teachers and myself are a part of the teaching and learning process. Because we write our own curriculum, I am involved in all meetings and work with teachers at the outset of the large units. This gives me information about what resources are needed as well as opportunities to help identify the logical places for information literacy standards to be addressed. Students in grades K–6 learn information literacy in the context of their curriculum and at their point of need, utilizing a variety of resources in different formats and from different sources. For example, in Team 3 (ages 8 to 10 years), one year the students do a geographic study of the regions of the United States, which they call "Journeys." The second year, they visit different countries of the world, which they call "Passports." We write our curriculum using the lenses of Basic School commonalities: response to aesthetics, sense of time and space, membership in groups, living with purpose, connections to nature, use of symbols. (A Basic School [Boyer, 1995] is a comprehensive plan for renewal for elementary schools based on the work of Ernest Boyer, bringing together all key components of an effective school and guided by four priorities: community, curriculum with coherence, a climate for learning, and a commitment to character.) In the Passports unit, the students study continents of the world with a focus on response to aesthetics. This kind of integrated, thematic, resource-based teaching and learning provides a very different experience from traditional studies. Objects in everyday living such as textiles, music, and folklore provide both a historical as well as contemporary view of their culture.

In addition to the resource-based curricular projects and units, our library media program provides resource-based support for literacy and the reading program. Every class in grades K–4 comes to the library media center weekly for literature/reading support. We strengthen the reading process by introducing students to excellent authors, illustrators, and experiences with all types of literature through our Media Literature Curriculum program. [Standard 5: The student who is an independent learner is information literate and appreciates literature and other creative expressions of information; AASL & AECT, 1998, 26.]

We are currently implementing a library media curriculum that identifies eight types of literature we want all Iowa City elementary students to experience with us at least twice in their years: historical fiction, poetry, biography, realistic fiction, fantasy, science fiction, nonfiction, and traditional literature. When the curriculum was developed, we designed lessons for each area outlining critical features and made bibliographies of three primary and three intermediate titles that represented what we considered the best of this type. In addition, we designed lessons for literary elements—plot, setting, character, theme, and point of view—as well as identified titles of note. At the end of the curriculum guide there are two examples of author study units. These provide a model for a media specialist or teacher to follow who might wish to provide an in-depth experience. The bibliographies help us all develop collections with a high standard. This is a very important and successful component of our instructional program. (Barbara Stein, personal communication, December 14, 1998)

INFORMATION LITERACY STANDARDS

In collaborating with the classroom teacher on a resource-based learning unit or any instructional lesson or project, the integration of information literacy standards is vital to the student's academic achievement. Information literacy involves the ability to access, evaluate, and use information to solve problems and pursue personal interests. Every library professional journal has at least one article on information literacy. State education departments across the nation have either created learning standards that address information literacy or are in the process of doing so. In addition, the American Association of School Librarians and the Association for Educational Communications and Technology have developed "Information Literacy Standards for Student Learning" found in *Information Power: Building Partnerships for Learning* (AASL & AECT, 1998, 8–44). These actions are in response to President Bush's call in 1989 to improve academic achievement for students in grades K–12 and to establish explicit goals or standards that specify what students should know and be able to do by the time they graduate from high school (Cross & Scott, 1997, 72).

Although all standards include information literacy, the connection with the library media program is implied rather than stated. As library media specialists, we must be proactive. Review the standards of your state, and identify those that have library media applications. If your state does not have standards yet, use the "Information Literacy Standards for Student Learning" as a framework (AASL & AECT, 1998, 8–44). Work as a member of the committee to revise the curriculum at the district or school level, and ensure that these information literacy standards are integrated into each content area while the curriculum is being developed. The likelihood that the standards will be integrated and that students will become information literate will be far greater if standards are integrated within individual subject areas. If this is not possible, go to the teachers, one individual or team at a time, and share the importance of integrating information literacy standards into the instructional program. Continue working with teachers until this is accomplished.

Using "Learning Standards for New York State," let's look at a sampling of standards from individual subject areas that demonstrates how pervasive information literacy standards are within this document and yet are not specifically labeled as such. Even though this is an example from just one state, you will be able to identify similar information literacy standards in your state documents as well (University of the State of New York, n.d., n.p.).

ENGLISH LANGUAGE ARTS

"Standard 1: Students will listen, speak, read, and write for information and understanding. As listeners and readers, students will collect data, facts, and ideas; discover relationships, concepts, and generalizations; and use knowledge generated from oral, written, and electronically produced texts. As speakers and writers, they will use oral and written language that follows the accepted conventions of the English language to acquire, interpret, apply, and transmit information."

SOCIAL STUDIES

"Standard 1: Students will use a variety of intellectual skills to demonstrate their understanding of major ideas, eras, themes, developments, and turning points in the history of the United States and New York."

MATHEMATICS, SCIENCE, AND TECHNOLOGY

"Standard 2: Students will access, generate, process, and transfer information using appropriate technologies."

CAREER DEVELOPMENT AND OCCUPATIONAL STUDIES

"Standard 3a: Students will demonstrate mastery of the foundation skills and competencies essential for success in the workplace." Under Elementary: "use ideas and information to make decisions and solve problems related to accomplishing a task."

HEALTH, PHYSICAL EDUCATION, AND HOME ECONOMICS

"Standard 2: Students will acquire the knowledge and ability necessary to create and maintain a safe and healthy environment."

In the example that follows, a media specialist participates as a curriculum partner in the collaborative planning, implementation, and assessment of a performance package, a large instructional unit used to assess Minnesota Graduation Standards. Mary Alice Anderson is the media/technology specialist at Winona Middle School (with an enrollment of 1,000 students) in Winona, Minnesota. Three seventh grade social studies teachers, and Mary Alice Anderson, agreed to work collaboratively on the preparation of a project entitled "The Expert Witness." They were asked to develop a unit that addresses the Minnesota Graduation Standard "People and Cultures."

Mary Alice and the social studies teachers spent over twelve hours writing the curriculum—identifying topics, selecting the best resources, and designing search forms for the students. They spent a half-day assessing the project as well. In addition, many other informal meetings took place as the unit was being implemented. Mary Alice and the teachers collaborated on the planning, content, activities, and assessment. Mary Alice describes the unit:

Students were expected to take a position on a current event or issue and to defend that position by demonstrating understanding of the history, facts, controversy, values, beliefs, and emotions surrounding the issue. Students were to prepare and present an oral testimony or a written summary of the event or issue chosen. The teacher's approval was required at several decision or check points throughout the process.

The research process took seven or eight days, alternating between the classroom and the media center. Classroom time was spent by students in organizing the information and meeting with the teacher concerning their progress. During their second or third visit to the media center, I provided instruction on resources that had been identified as being especially useful. Note taking and bibliographic skills were stressed. In addition, throughout the unit I saw opportunities to address other appropriate information literacy standards in conjunction with the "People and Cultures" standard. I also provided students with a search strategy form that they used to brainstorm ideas, record sources, and take notes. The total project took three weeks to complete.

A rubric was developed during the planning stage and was distributed to students at the outset of the unit. Students were assessed on all phases of the project: both the process the students used as well as their product and final presentation. Feedback forms were completed by the teacher for each student's oral or written presentation.

This project is just one example of the impact the Minnesota Graduation Standards and performance packages have had on the middle school media program. This package, as with many others, is highly dependent on access to information in all formats. Opportunities to teach and reinforce information literacy are implicit throughout the teaching and learning process. Opportunities for collaboration have increased along with the demand for resources. As teachers develop and implement the packages, they are more attuned to the need for thoughtful and collaborative planning, teaching appropriate developmental and search skills, and assessing both student work and the teaching and learning process. Students often feel overwhelmed with the intensity of the packages, but as they become accustomed to the engaged, authentic learning typical of the packages, they will continue to acquire the information literacy abilities that are part of becoming a successful student and lifelong learner. The teachers felt this package was very successful and will assign it again with ongoing modifications developed during the evaluation session. (Mary Alice Anderson, personal communication, May 16, 1999)

CONCLUSION

It is in the library media center—the center of the instructional program—that students will learn in the 21st century. It is here that students will utilize resources to learn both the content and information literacy standards, or lifelong learning skills, that will make them information-literate as well as successful adults.

Although there are school and district policies that may drive staffing, budget, selection, facilities, and other areas, thereby impacting on the quality of program, your leadership as well as the partnerships you develop with both your principal and classroom teachers will overcome many challenges. By developing these partnerships, we are building a support system, a network of advocates in the learning community. These individuals understand and appreciate the contributions of the library media program to student learning, and they will become its advocate. This three-way partnership, developed through your leadership, will redefine the instructional program.

Program Implementation and Assessment: Redefining the Instructional Program

6

The last two steps in instructional design are implementation and assessment completing the process begun in the previous chapter. Included within this chapter are an overview of four information search processes, a discussion of technology as a learning tool, and various strategies that will help classroom teachers and library media specialists better meet the needs of students. There is a wealth of information from which the selection of these models and strategies has been made. It is a highly selective list. It represents those models and strategies that have the greatest potential for positive impact on the implementation and assessment of both the instructional and the library media programs. Examples are from library media specialists who demonstrate how they have translated theory into practice. The section on assessment provides an overview of the process as it is evolving and illustrates how the library media specialist functions as a curriculum partner within the process.

PROGRAM IMPLEMENTATION

One of the main challenges facing library media specialists is to help students be successful in accessing, evaluating, and using information in relation to their instructional and personal needs—in thinking critically about a topic, organizing ideas, and solving problems. Teaching a research process or information search process, which is a primary function of the library media program, will help students accomplish this.

The Research Process

Research is a process that students begin using before they enter school. If a child at the zoo asks about a bear, and the parent or guardian shares information about that animal, in essence the child has been involved in research. When a child enters kindergarten and wants more information about bears, a teacher, library media specialist, or parent volunteer may look up "bears" in a book or print or electronic encyclopedia and share the information with the child. This child has participated in the research process.

In primary grades, when students are inquisitive or have personal or academic questions, they are introduced to research through simple graphic organizers. A graphic organizer is a mental map that helps students classify knowledge by organizing individual pieces of information into a holistic conceptual framework. This helps students focus on what they want to learn and assists them in remembering the information easily. The student can then analyze, interpret, and draw conclusions concerning the information (Strong, 1997, 18). Even though children are introduced to graphic organizers in the primary grades, students continue to use some of the same tools into high school and beyond. Initially children participate in the process as a member of a class with the assistance of the teacher. As they gain experience, they use organizers independently to begin their individual research and solve curricular problems. Although there are many graphic organizers, the following discussion explores three as examples of mental maps.

A *Web* is particularly helpful in analyzing traits. For instance, the name of an animal is placed in the center of the Web within a circle. Lines are drawn emanating from the center circle on which students list types of animals such as bears, tigers, and elephants. Students then draw a circle around each type of animal and develop questions about each for which they wish to find answers. Now that they know what they want to learn, students—as a class, small cooperative group, or individually—can begin to find answers in resources available in the library media center, classroom, public library, or home.

The *KWL model* begins with a topic about which students want more information. They list information about the topic in columns. In the first column, they record everything they already know (K) about the topic. In the next column, they record everything they want (W) to learn. In the last column, after the lesson or the research, students record what they have learned (L).

The *Venn diagram* is especially helpful in comparing and contrasting characteristics. For example, using two large intersecting circles, students list all characteristics of desert animals in one circle and those of the rain forest in the other. In the section where the two circles overlap, students list characteristics or attributes the animals have in common.

More formal paths for the research process are used by elementary through high school students and can be adapted for the grade, maturity, and involvement level desired. The graphic organizers will continue to be an important element of the research process. Four examples of research paths or processes are discussed in the following sections. Each is an excellent model that can be adopted as a districtwide information search process or used in an individual school.

Teaching the Library Research Process, by Carol Kuhlthau (1994b), provides a comprehensive and sequential process for gathering and using information when given a research assignment. It is founded in the writings and research of John Dewey, Jerome Bruner, and George Kelly, major Constructivists (iv, viii).

There are seven stages in the Library Research Process:

1. Initiating a Research Assignment
2. Selecting a Topic
3. Exploring Information
4. Forming a Focus
5. Collecting Information
6. Preparing to Present
7. Assessing the Process

Each stage includes the *task*, the *thoughts* students will have as they proceed, the *feelings* they may experience during the process, the *actions* they must take, and the *strategies* they may use. This model is unique in that it addresses the feelings students experience during a research project and helps them manage this part of the process.

An overview of the first stage of the research process is used as an example of the steps included in each stage.

Initiating a Research Assignment

- *Task*: The student's task in the first stage is to prepare to select a topic. The student must understand what is required of him as well as the expectations of the assignment. The prior experience of the student will determine how he approaches this new responsibility.

- *Thoughts*: The student will think about the assignment, ask questions, and gain an understanding of the task; he will try to relate it to prior experiences and learning, and he will consider possible topics.

- *Feelings*: When a teacher assigns a research project, a student may feel a sense of apprehension and uncertainty concerning both the task and the outcome. As the student gains more information, these feelings should decrease.

- *Actions*: The student may talk with others about the task, browse through the library media collection—print and technology, and write down questions about prospective topics.

- *Strategies*: The student may brainstorm, discuss the options with friends, think about possible topics, and be willing to tolerate some uncertainty at this point in the process. (Kuhlthau, 1994b, 1–3)

Students are active participants with the teacher and library media specialist in the last stage of the process: assessment. Both the students' self-assessment and the teacher and library media specialist's evaluations will help students improve their research process skills and apply them to future research assignments (Kuhlthau, 1994a, 59).

Beatrice Baaden, library media specialist at Packard Middle School (with approximately 700 students) in the Plainedge School District, North Massapequa, New York, has used Kuhlthau's research process for many years. She describes the progression students at Packard follow as they use the information search process:

In sixth grade, we introduce them to the library media center as well as the school through an information search process project. It is an exciting project on "Ancient Civilizations," and students get to know the library media center and become comfortable in its environment. We identify the appropriate standards and blend these with the curriculum content. Because this is the student's first experience in using a research process, we begin to work in the first three stages: initiating the research assignment, selecting a topic, and exploring the information. As a first step, students select a topic but not before they learn "how" to choose one. They review a general topic list and think about what they already know as well as what they would like to learn more about, what is important to them, where this knowledge came from, why they are thinking this way, and what two or three topics they want to further investigate; read about these topics; and talk with other students, teachers, and myself. Students may indicate that they have decided on their topic, but the teachers and myself encourage them not to make hasty decisions and to further reflect on the two or three topics in which they are really interested. Students' language begins to change from "I have chosen a topic" to "Maybe I will investigate . . ." Their change in language is indicative of what is going on in their heads.

Once they finally select their topic, they explore a wide variety of resources to locate information, both print and technology. Students take notes and begin to create an annotated bibliography, assessing how useful specific resources are to their particular topic. This type of critical thinking is very important. Specific directions presented to each student guide them through this process. Students also are required to complete an outline from which they will make an oral presentation. The English Language Arts teachers assist students to organize their outline. The final stage in this first assignment is to create an oral presentation.

In seventh grade, students progress to creating a research paper, using all stages of the research process. This Zoology unit includes science, English, library media, and technology. Early in this multidisciplinary project, students receive directions for the unit, checklists, and a rubric that gives them clear direction for the expectations of the unit. Students can select any animal, except a domesticated one, and develop questions for research, write a poem, and select a graphic image related to their topic downloaded from the Internet. We build on what was learned from the Ancient Civilizations unit and require that students develop a focus as well as write a focus statement. This focus statement drives the research paper. We have found that students much before seventh grade have difficulty doing this.

After their focus is formed and their statement accepted, students progress to the next stages of collecting information, preparing their report, and participating in the assessment of both the research process as well as their product.

In eighth grade, the major unit for which students use the research process is Earth Science. Students participate in an independent scientific research project involving a controlled experiment in the fields of geology, meteorology, oceanography, or astronomy. Students have had two years' experience using the research process and will be involved in the rigor and reality of scientific research. By relating the research process to the scientific process, students learn that these processes are very similar. First, students choose a topic as a result of extensive reading and reflecting on several possibilities, design and implement original experiments utilizing scientific manipulation and the use of statistics, and prove or disprove a hypothesis that they develop. Students receive clear directions, a timeline of the research process, checklists, and a rubric.

Just before students declare their hypothesis for acceptance by their teacher, we offer three reflection seminars: one on resource selection, another on statistics, and finally, a seminar on the rubric. Then students write the remainder of the paper. (Beatrice Baaden, personal communication, June 7, 1999)

All three projects are excellent and involve students actively in their learning.

Brainstorms and Blueprints: Teaching Library Research as a Thinking Process, by Barbara K. Stripling and Judy M. Pitts (1988), "provides creative strategies (brainstorms) and logical processes (blueprints)" to assist secondary teachers and library media specialists in creating library media research assignments for students. The process provides direction for teaching the research process as a thinking skill.

The steps in the research process are as follows:

1. Choose a broad topic.
2. Get an overview of the topic.
3. Narrow the topic.
4. Develop a thesis or statement of purpose.

5. Formulate questions to guide research.

6. Plan for research and production.

7. Find/Analyze/Evaluate sources.

8. Evaluate evidence/Take notes/Compile bibliography.

9. Establish conclusions/Organize information into an outline.

10. Create and present final product. (Stripling & Pitts, 1988, 20)

As students begin to narrow their topic and work through each of the remaining steps, ideas on which students should reflect are identified. Reflection is emphasized throughout this process.

Sarah Roberson, library media specialist at Fayetteville High School Library (grades 10–12, with an enrollment of approximately 1,500 students), Fayetteville School District, in Fayetteville, Arkansas, describes a project with Advanced Placement Language and Composition students in which the *Brainstorms and Blueprints* research process is used:

Students' choice of topics is broad: from world burial practices to chaos theory to George Lucas's use of mythology. The project is graded as heavily on process as on product.

One of the first lessons the library media specialists teach is how to evaluate reference books. This exercise not only allows students to gain or sharpen a valuable skill, but the presentation given by each student on a reference work gives all students a look at a broad range of topic ideas. Within a day of finishing presentations, students have settled on a broad topic and are doing overview reading to help narrow their topics. One of the strengths of this model is the emphasis on reflection beginning at this first step and continuing throughout the process.

Their next process grade is based on a well-written thesis and questions. Students are instructed on writing questions and setting up notesheets based on these questions, but many choose the notecard method.

Although organization is stressed throughout by both library media specialists and classroom teachers, actual planning for research is not approached as a formal step, and therefore students often omit this step. As a result, many flounder for a while as they begin to find resources, but almost all settle into a fairly productive method. At the point at which our students begin locating resources, a lesson on evaluating sources (with more emphasis on Internet sources each year) is taught.

Of course, the most exciting part of the project comes when students begin questioning the information they have located to see if it is consistent from source to source, if it is adequate, and what conclusions it leads them to. After several days in our library media center, we accompany students to the nearby University of Arkansas Library, where they expand their search in a larger collection.

As we return from that last day of intensive locating, students begin putting the pieces together: outlining, drafting, peer editing, redrafting, submitting to teachers for an initial reading, redrafting again, tracking down incomplete bibliographic sources, and putting the finishing steps on a project that has often consumed their lives for more than a month. (Sarah Roberson, personal communication, October 8, 1999)

Also contained in the model are six levels of REACTS: A Taxonomy of Research Reactions that provides teachers with ideas that will generate original thinking on the part of students in the creation of a product. Included below are three of the six levels of the model, with one example of a possible assignment at each level that is designed to produce creative thought. It helps delineate the gradual progression of students to the use of higher levels of thinking skills by the activities developed for them. Stripling presents these ideas:

Level 2: Explaining

> Students recall and restate, summarize, or paraphrase information. They find examples, explain events or actions. Students understand the information well enough to be able to put it in a new context.
>
> > *Show* the events of your research on a map, and explain the importance of each event.

Level 4: Challenging

> Students make critical judgments about their subject based on internal or external standards. (Standard may be student's own, or teacher or class may decide criteria. "I didn't like it" or "I don't believe it" are not enough.)
>
> > Act as an attorney and *argue* to punish or acquit a historical character or a country for a crime or misdeed.

Level 6: Synthesizing

> Students create an entirely original product based on a new concept or theory.
>
> > *Devise* an ethical code for present-day researchers or scientists that could regulate their activities in a particular field. (1994b, 109–114)

"The Box" as described by Marjorie Rohrbach in Chapter 5 in the section on Collaboration comes from the REACTS model for thinking for secondary research experiences.

"The Big6TM" by Michael B. Eisenberg and Robert E. Berkowitz (1990), found in *Information Problem-Solving: The Big Six Skills Approach to Library & Information Skills Instruction* (1990), presents a research process based on Bloom's Taxonomy of cognitive objectives that provides a strategy or systematic approach to meeting information needs (Eisenberg & Berkowitz, 1992, 99). The process blends an information literacy curriculum with an information problem-solving and critical thinking model taught in the context of the instructional program (Eisenberg & Berkowitz, 1990, xxvii). The process is applicable to academic as well as personal problem-

solving tasks and is adaptable to any content area as well as grade level (Eisenberg & Berkowitz, 1990, 1). Eisenberg and Johnson (1996) use "the Big6" to help students become technology literate as well as information literate (1–8). Although it is described in six steps, it is not necessarily sequential.

These steps are described within a broad, problem-solving context:

1. *Task Definition*: Getting a clear understanding of the problem that needs to be solved includes the questions to be answered and the kinds of information needed.

2. *Information Seeking Strategies*: Selecting the best sources to solve the problem in an information-rich climate can be challenging, but using criteria such as accuracy, reliability, and availability will help narrow the large amount of resources.

3. *Location and Access*: Implementing the information seeking strategy involves being able to locate and use access tools such as print and nonprint indexes as well as being able to search and locate information in online catalogs and on the Internet.

4. *Use of Information*: In this step students evaluate the information, which requires them to read, hear, view, touch, listen, extract relevant information, take notes, and cite sources in context and for a bibliography.

5. *Synthesis*: Organizing and presenting the information, which is the application of the relevant information learned to the information problem, requires that the student restructure the information to create a new product, select the most appropriate format for the presentation, and effectively communicate the solution to the problem.

6. *Evaluation*: Examining both the problem-solving process and the product to determine the student's success in completing the task involves reflecting on the process and product to determine the strengths and areas of need as well as the amount of time spent to solve the problem. Students interact with the teacher and library media specialist in this last step of the process, receiving feedback on process and product while critically evaluating their information problem-solving process (Eisenberg & Berkowitz, 1990, 5–9).

A unit developed in collaboration among Gail Bush, curriculum librarian, Merrilee Andersen Kwielford, technology librarian, and an English III teacher from the Maine West High School (grades 9–12 with an enrollment of 1900 students) in Des Plaines, Illinois, uses "the Big6" research process as a foundation. This exemplary unit demonstrates the ease with which teachers and students use the process.

The teacher initiated the collaboration with the library media specialists on a unit about the Vietnam War. This unit was designed in preparation for reading *The Things They Carried* by Tom O'Brien. The process is described by both library media specialists. Bush begins:

The teacher wanted students to not only access, evaluate, and use information as well as learn appropriate information skills in pursuit of their topic on Vietnam, but also to create a multimedia presentation about their topic to be presented to members of their classroom using PowerPoint presentation software.

The teacher met initially with Merrilee and myself to discuss the purpose of the research project and to develop a list of topics as well as activities to address specific information literacy standards. Once the standards were identified, the teacher created the rubric to evaluate both the process and the final product, which was shared with the students. It was decided that students would work as partners; choose one of the topics from the list; identify questions related to this topic; locate, access, and evaluate information as to its usefulness for their topic and take notes from the information sources as well as develop a bibliography; create a PowerPoint presentation, synthesizing what they had learned about their topic by putting the information in outline form, as well as being prepared to give an oral presentation using the slides they prepared in the Tech Center; and self-evaluate their work in conjunction with the teacher and library media specialists using the rubric prepared by the teacher.

At the beginning of the research, I presented an overview of "the Big6" research process that had been adopted by Maine West High School for all student research. However, I presented an in-depth summary of "location and access" of information pertinent to students' particular topics including use of the Internet. As students progressed through "the Big6" stages of their research, both the teacher and myself provided guidance and instruction as needed. Students also received a "Checklist" that identified several information sources that each partnership should access including such tools as: periodical indexes, electronic encyclopedias, books, and printed material as well as tasks that needed to be completed such as: organizing notes, preparing an outline, developing a bibliography, devising three test questions about their topic, and making a decision about who would discuss which slides in the PowerPoint presentation.

Kwielford continues the story:

The teacher scheduled two days in the upstairs library for students to complete their research and create an outline of their topic; and two days in the Tech Center, downstairs, to produce their presentations using PowerPoint to create at least five slides with at least three different formats and at least one relevant picture or graphic from the Internet. I instructed students on the use of PowerPoint.

The projects were completed in approximately one week with presentations to follow. Students who needed more time in the LRC or in the Tech Center came in before and after school, during lunch or free periods. Students learned new information literacy standards as well as practicing others, participated in an authentic learning experience, and were active members in their own learning as they accessed, used, and then presented their learning for others. (Gail Bush and Merrilee Kwielford, personal communication, June 23, 1999)

Pathways to Knowledge, by Marjorie L. Pappas and Ann E. Tepe (1997), is a research process based in the learning theories of Piaget, Dewey, and

Vygotsky and is congruent with the Constructivists' way of approaching learning. Using this nonlinear, holistic information process model, students employ various strategies and skills to access, evaluate, and use information. Students are able to enter the process at different stages to begin their search, using the one that is most appropriate for their instructional need.

The Pathways Model delineates the following stages:

- *Appreciation*: As students appreciate the world around them, they are often motivated to initiate a discovery phase of the search process; appreciation can occur in any stage of the model.

- *Presearch*: Beginning their search by using a graphic organizer, students make connections between their prior knowledge and their information need, developing strategies that help them create an overview and describe a focus for their search.

- *Search*: Using information providers, resources, and tools, students identify relevant information and then plan and implement their search strategy.

- *Interpretation*: Through the processes of analyzing, synthesizing, and evaluating information that is most useful and relevant to their need, students reflect on and interpret the information, and then construct personal meaning and knowledge.

- *Communication*: Students plan, create, and present a product representative of their new knowledge or learning, and in an appropriate format.

- *Evaluation*: Evaluation by the student, peers, and the teacher is ongoing throughout the research process, assessing both the process and the product. (Pappas & Tepe, 1997, 5–8)

Gayle A. Geitgey has been the library media specialist for the past twenty-five years at Urbana High School (with an enrollment of 670 students), Urbana City Schools, in Urbana, Ohio. Most recently, Gayle has been the district media specialist and technology coordinator for this small city school district serving 20,000 students. The Pathways Model, which has been adopted by the district, has been used at the high school for approximately five years.

One of the instructional partnerships that Gayle has established is described in the extract that follows. Gayle reports:

The computer applications teacher and myself created a project in which we teamed to teach, facilitate, and assess student performance. Students were required to do a research project on any aspect of technology culminating in the creation of a Web page, which should communicate the knowledge they gained. At the outset of the project, they were expected to make decisions about how their learnings would be shared with peers and how products that they created would be assessed. There were five classes of approximately twenty students each, with each class deciding on a different method of presentation as well as assessment. One of the classes decided that they would work in partners to complete the project and would use a rubric to assess the process, product, and presentation. Students created the rubric with the guidance of the teacher. We used the assessment from the previous year to modify and improve the process for this year. The Pathways Model guided all of us through the process.

When introducing the project, the teacher shared his appreciation for technology and how it had changed his life. Although students initially had a hard time thinking about a topic for which they might have an appreciation or about which they wanted to know more, we started the research process with the Presearch stage. Many high school students resist working through presearch because they have been using webbing throughout their school career and feel that this is no longer necessary. However, students began to formulate questions and then brainstorm possible topics using the KWL [what they *know, what* they want to learn, and what they *learned*] chart. They created a new chart for each topic they were considering. This helps them make the final choice of topic.

We then moved onto the Search stage, where we worked on the types of search strategies and how to use a search engine correctly. We investigated the four search strategies: explore, browse, hierarchical, and analytical. Although we touched on all the search strategies, we really emphasized the Browse and Analytical modes.

Students finished their research using both print and technology sources, including the Internet, and then organized their information, integrated concepts, analyzed them in relation to the problem of creating Web pages, created their Web page as well as a report on their topic, and, finally, prepared their presentations, which were shared with members of their class using an LCD projector. Students received the rubric at the beginning and referred to it often during the project. The teacher and myself provided feedback to students throughout the process. While students assessed their own process, product and presentation, they participated in the assessment of these elements for other students as well. The teacher and myself evaluated all three elements of the project for each student and shared this with them. By the time the project was complete, students felt very positive about the new knowledge they gained. (Gayle Geitgey, personal communication, July 2, 1999)

The authors of these four research processes have made a significant contribution to the information literacy of students. The processes are excellent search models based on "Bloom's Taxonomy of the Cognitive Domain: Knowledge, Comprehension, Application, Analysis, Synthesis, and Evaluation" (in Bloom, 1956, 201–207). School districts or schools should evaluate these models and endorse one to be used throughout a student's instructional career. The library media specialist can be a catalyst in this process. It is through the continuing use of a research process beginning in pre-kindergarten that students learn to apply essential problem-solving and critical thinking skills to authentic learning experiences. In this way, students develop the skills necessary to become independent lifelong learners.

Technology, Teachers, and the Library Media Specialist

Although discussion of technology has been integrated throughout this text, it is necessary to discuss technology as a unique and essential learning tool in the implementation of an effective library media program. We must become proficient in its use, help classroom teachers use and integrate it into their instructional programs, collaborate with teachers on instructional programs in which students will utilize technology as one of their resources, and ultimately become the technology specialist in our building. Unless we do this, someone else will fill this role and eventually we will be regarded as expendable.

An analysis from the Educational Testing Service on the 1996 National Assessment of Educational Progress fourth and eighth grade mathematics tests gives a rationale for why media specialists must assume this role, and as soon as possible. The analysis suggests that students whose teachers received technology training scored higher than their counterparts whose teachers had not received training. The contrast was significant at the eighth grade, where there was a difference of 35 percent of a grade level (Archer, 1998, 11). This formidable documentation should motivate each of us to become a technology specialist and a trainer of teachers.

Impact of Technology on Library Media Programs

The Internet, "the worldwide 'network of networks'," the "electronic superhighway" (Summers, 1996, 21), has revolutionized the way we think about and access information. While it is constantly growing, it is not organized or easily accessed by the novice. But the world is becoming more and more dependent on information accessible on the Internet. It is comprised of local area networks (LANs) as well as international networks. No library media center can provide all the information students will require to complete their education. Technology, including the Internet, provides access to the world, enabling students to learn and search while sitting in their school's media center or at home (Summers, 1996, 21).

Library media specialists at electronic library media centers must acquire new skills in computer networking, collection development, database maintenance, information input, and searching catalogs and databases, as well as have experience with a broad range of online systems (Blake, 1996, 13). Let us look at how technology is presently impacting, and will continue to impact at an even more rapid rate in the future, the roles of the library media specialist.

As *information specialist*, we have traditionally been the managers of information in a school. Teachers and students knew that if they had an information question, we would be able to link resources with their information need. Today and in the future, we must engender this same confidence in our ability to manage technology resources, including the Internet, in the same manner.

Because of the wealth of information, there is a need for someone to organize and codify it for teachers and students. Educational reform requires students to think critically and evaluate the validity and appropriateness of the tremendous volume of information that is available. Both these needs address the role of the library media specialist as information specialist managing resources (Berger, 1998, 6). We must become experts in utilizing the Internet and the World Wide Web: become Web masters, the person who manages its resources by creating home pages and contributing to the knowledge base of the Internet; evaluating Web sites for accuracy, authority, and content; selecting the most appropriate Web sites and aligning them with the curriculum and standards; linking these sites to the home page, thereby helping make the Web more easily accessible to and usable by teachers and students in solving information problems—reducing the time spent locating the information, and more time evaluating and using it; and becoming familiar with products that will assist us in achieving this goal (Berger, 1998, x, 5). We must become master managers of the Internet, evaluating and organizing resources just as we have evaluated and organized print and other nonprint resources.

The collection, including emerging technologies, must be developed and maintained at the school level. Although library media centers provide access to (1) resources beyond the library doors through interlibrary loan, and (2) the volume of resources available on the Internet, budgets must be sufficient to provide not only current and heavily used print and technology resources but also necessary hardware. Although schools will be able to develop a more focused local library media collection because of access to interlibrary loan and the Internet, it is the responsibility of each school district to provide the resources that will ensure that students become both information literate and technology literate (Blake, 1996, 11). Resources must be available to enable students to achieve their information literacy goals.

As *teacher and instructional partner*, the library media specialist has an opportunity to be a major player in developing and teaching the effective and efficient use of technology, the person who assists teachers and students to become technology literate. We must be a full curriculum partner with the classroom teacher in the development, implementation, and assessment of the instructional program. We must find many opportunities to teach teachers how to access, evaluate, and integrate technology resources into their curriculum so that they can navigate the Web and use it effectively. Through informal staff development with one teacher at a time, or more formally with a larger group, we must teach and train teachers to use all library media resources, including the Internet, effectively and efficiently.

Whereas traditionally we taught students how to access and use resources, today we must help them to think critically as well, as we teach them to access, evaluate, and use all library media resources including the Internet. We must help them identify strategies to select appropriate resources; teach them information literacy in the context of the instructional program; and assist them in making connections or links from information they have searched to create new knowledge based on their past understandings. We must teach students how to evaluate Web sites for accuracy, authority, and content; how to use search engines, directories, and bookmarks effectively (Berger, 1998, 6).

Sally Tower, library media specialist at Hutchinson Central Technical High School (grades 9–12) with an enrollment of approximately 1,150 students in the Buffalo Public Schools, Buffalo, New York, cautions that we address the socialization of students as we collaborate with teachers:

Ensuring that students are involved in instructional activities with other students and teachers and not withdrawn from their peers by interacting with a computer or machine is critical. When designing instructional programs, we need to work with teachers to guarantee that students will be involved in cooperative learning activities, debates, role plays, discussion groups, and peer tutoring that encourages positive student interaction. I am concerned that some students are spending an inordinate amount of time on Internet Web sites, drawing conclusions from information that may have little or no authority. As technology becomes more pervasive in our lives, we need to provide many opportunities in the context of the instructional program for socialization with peers. This is an integral component of a healthy climate of a school. (Sally Tower, personal communication, June 7, 1999)

Mary Alice Anderson, media specialist as well as technology specialist at Winona Middle School, in Winona, Minnesota, provided both informal and formal staff development on all technology tools for staff members in her school. As a result of her expertise and knowledge, she has become the technology staff development coordinator for her district. All programs focus on Minnesota Graduation Performance standards. She maintains:

Providing staff development at the school and district level is probably the most important thing we can do. Technology is so critical. Teachers realize how important it is and are willing to learn. They are very responsive. During this past year, programs were offered at the district level on many topics. Those that follow are a few examples: "Internet Search Engines"; "Classroom Hyperstudio Projects"; "Critical Use of the Internet"; and "Integrating Technology and Information Literacy into the Curriculum." If we want technology to be used effectively as a tool, we must teach and demonstrate how it can be integrated into the context of teacher's programs. (Mary Alice Anderson, personal communication, May 16, 1999)

As *program administrator*, we must take the lead in developing policies about information access of the Internet and the ethical and social responsibility concerning its use. The ALA Bill of Rights, ALA Resolutions on filtering software, and other documents should be reviewed as these policies are developed (Berger, 1998, x). In addition, we must function as a leader, keeping current on emerging technologies and concepts as well as continually sharing these with colleagues through journal articles, books, Web sites, and other resources that will help them continue to learn and be open to new suggestions and change. As a leader, we are continually revisiting our library media vision with our library media advisory committee and making necessary adjustments.

If you do not feel you are a technology specialist, you must take courses and work with a mentor to assume this role. Schools of library and information science must provide courses to prepare library media specialists to function in this role, which is being redefined by technology. These schools must also assist those who are presently in library media positions.

Peter Milbury, library media specialist at Chico High School Library, in Chico, California, demonstrates all roles as both a technology specialist and a leader. In 1990, through the support of his principal, Peter Milbury became the first teacher in his high school to obtain Internet access through an account with CORE, the California Online Resources for Education, for California's public schools. He started at a time when there were few Internet resources available for K–12 schools and almost no resources to guide him in its use. However, he was able to regularly log on to CORE to explore what was available. His interest grew as he saw its potential. He soon moved his desk with the computer and modem to the center of the reading room. This gave him an opportunity to tell others about the information he was learning from the Internet (Milbury, 1996, 107–112).

Milbury soon began to download information and share it with teachers and administrators. As he gained confidence and more resources became available that were applicable to students and the curriculum, he began to offer an occasional workshop. These grew until he was providing regular training sessions on the Internet for all his school staff and others in the district (Milbury, 1996, 107–112).

As teachers and departments became knowledgeable about its potential, the use of the Internet grew. Milbury's goal was to involve as many teachers and classes in the Internet as possible. At the time, he was concerned that most of the resources were not user friendly and that teachers did not have time or expertise to search each system or network. Although tremendous advances have taken place since that time and resources have become more user friendly, because the information on the Internet has expanded exponentially many teachers still do not have the time or expertise to access and evaluate the sites applicable to their curricular area (Milbury, 1996, 107–112).

In 1998, eight years after he began to explore the Internet and help others do the same, Milbury is creating home pages on the Web and contributing to its knowledge base. He engages teachers in the use of technology through a variety of strategies. He always keeps his time on the Internet and creation of Web pages focused on the curriculum through collaboration with teachers. As a result of classes that he offers on the Internet and other related technology software, he has gained the confidence of teachers. They recognize him not only as an expert in the use of technology but also as a friend providing opportunities to collaborate on the instructional program (Milbury, 1998, 40, 41).

Other ideas he shares for collaboration include a "Web-memo" that he is able to adapt to individual teachers. For example, Milbury may send a Web-memo to a teacher with copies of Web pages he has just linked to the library media center's home page asking for an opinion on the resources. In the memo he may reference the area of the "Chico High School [CHS] Library Helpful Bookmarks" where he has placed the link, or he may include a copy of the home page showing the link. He uses the CHS home page, the Web-memo, e-mail messages, the daily bulletin, and any other available tool to keep teachers informed about the resources and services in the library media center. He sends copies to the principal to keep him informed as well (Milbury, 1998, 40, 41).

The following experience is descriptive of the type of service Milbury provides. A teacher came to the library media center to brainstorm ideas for a brief lesson on "symbolism." Because Milbury knew he did not have enough print resources to support research for several classes, he suggested that they browse the Internet. They found several sources that were helpful: "The Symbolism Dictionary," which had its own keyword search engine with an alphabetical index; and the online holdings of the Fine Arts Museums of San Francisco. Milbury linked both these sites to the Chico High School Web site. He suggested that students look up a word symbol and then compare it to a painting found by keyword searching in the online holdings of the Fine Arts Museums source. The teacher agreed with the suggestion and completed his lesson design by requiring that students write about the meaning of "symbol" and then present their learning to the class. When students came to the library media center, Milbury demonstrated how to get to these two links on the library Web site. Because of the visual nature of the assignment, some students used PowerPoint software available on the library media center local area network as well as the LCD projection system to develop their final presentations (Milbury, 1998, 40, 41).

Milbury has been successful because of his expertise in technology as well as his ability to provide needed information and skills for teachers and staff through both informal and formal staff development opportunities. He collaborates with teachers in nonthreatening and supportive situations to integrate technology into the curriculum while helping these colleagues to become comfortable and competent in its effective use. He is always working to expand on the mutual respect and trust he has developed with members of the learning community. Finally, he is a leader. He has a vision for how the Internet should be used; he is drawing one teacher at a time, informally, to the computer; and he is seeing these people share their accomplishments with others who in turn come for assistance.

Resources to Help You Become a Technology Specialist

As technology impacts our role, we must identify resources that will maintain our expertise as technology specialists and enable us to help teachers use technology effectively. Many books have been written about technology and telecommunications, whole volumes of professional journals are devoted to this issue, and there are Web sites that will guide you through the process. The understanding and use of each resource in the selective list that follows are critical in your pursuit of becoming a technology specialist.

Internet for Active Learners: Curriculum-Based Strategies for K–12, by Pam Berger (1998), in just eight chapters provides practical information on the Internet, including Internet tools, how to evaluate Web sites, how to integrate the Internet into the curriculum, how to develop a home page, preparing the reader to teach the Internet to others, and resources that actively involve students. This is a valuable tool that is easy to understand. It includes many Web sites exemplifying specific concepts presented.

ICONnect on the Web is another outstanding source of information. It is a technology initiative created and maintained by AASL. ICONnect includes learning opportunities on the Internet for teachers, library media specialists, students, and parents. Its goal is to support school library media specialists to assume leadership roles in using the Internet. Following are the resources that comprise ICONnect. Visit ICONnect on the Web at <http://www.ala.org/ICONN/>.

KidsConnect is a reference service providing assistance to students in grades K–12 with questions concerning the Internet. This initiative is supported by library media specialists from throughout the world. Through electronic mail, students contact the main KidsConnect address and receive a message from a volunteer library media specialist with assistance within two days. Visit <http://www.ala.org/ICONN/kidsconn.html>.

FamiliesConnect provides an introduction to the Internet where parents and children can learn about and use it together. There is a five-lesson course on the Internet, a list of the ten top Internet sites for families, and information on information literacy for parents. Visit <http://www.ala.org/ICONN/familiesconnect.html>.

Online courses provide teachers and library media specialists with direction on how to use the Internet to make curriculum connections and answer technology questions. There are basic and advanced courses. Examples of these free courses include: Integrating the Internet into Elementary Curriculum; Developing Content for Your Home Page; Search Engines; and Telecollaborative Activities on the Net. Topics change as new needs are identified. Visit <http://www.ala.org/ICONN/onlineco.html>.

Learning Space or Virtual Office is an innovative environment designed as a learning laboratory for interactive online courses, meetings, field trips, and events. It allows library media specialists to participate in "virtual environments while they learn how to successfully navigate, collaborate, and work." Visit <http://www.ala.org/ICONN/v_office.html>.

ICONnectPublications includes information on the latest resources concerning the internet such as *Internet for Active Learners* by Pam Berger (1998), strategies for integrating the Internet into the curriculum, Web sites of curriculum projects that encourage students to become active learners, and information to develop an Internet workshop for teachers. Visit <http://www.ala.org/ICONN/i_pubs.html>.

IC Prize for Collaboration through Technology encourages the use of the Internet in outstanding curriculum-based units collaboratively planned by teachers and library media specialists. Several grants are awarded each year to teacher/library media specialist partnerships showing excellent curriculum units. Visit <http://www.ala.org/ICONN/icprize.html>.

LM_NET, an electronic mail discussion group, and AskERIC, an online help and referral service, are the last resources in this selective list. LM-NET, which is a listserv for school library media specialists worldwide, was created to assist library media specialists in the implementation of program as well as to make better use of the Internet. This e-mail discussion group was developed by Dr. Michael Eisenberg, then at Syracuse University in New York State and director of the ERIC Clearinghouse on Information and Technology, and Peter Milbury, then Pleasant Valley High School library media specialist, Chico, California (Eisenberg & Milbury, 1996, 32). Library media specialists at all levels who subscribe to this service can participate in discussions on school library topics such as: leadership, the principal, flexible scheduling, budget, staff development, facilities, collaboration, student access to the Internet, advocacy, or any other school library issue. LM_NET is accessed on the Web through electronic mail. To subscribe, send a message to <LISTSERV@LISTSERV.SYR.EDU>. Then send the command <SUBSCRIBE LM_NET> followed by your first and last name, in that order (Eisenberg & Milbury, 1996, 47–49).

The goal of AskERIC is to provide assistance for K–12 educators—teachers, library media specialists, and administrators—in acquiring needed information while learning to use the Internet effectively. AskERIC is sponsored by ERIC, the Educational Resources Information Center, which is a program of the U.S. Department of Education and the largest source of information on education. The advantage of this program is that an individual will interact with the person seeking information to clarify the need and then assist in the selection and delivery of the information within forty-eight hours. The AskERIC staff member will identify a variety of resources from both the ERIC system and the Internet. To contact the question service, send your request by electronic mail to <askeric@ericir.syr.edu>. To use the AskERIC Electronic Library, Gopher to <ericir.syr.edu> (Eisenberg & Milbury, 1996, 47–49).

These resources will help the library media specialist who is new to technology and telecommunications become informed and learn to use the Web effectively. Those who are proficient Internet users are probably already subscribers to LM_NET and using AskERIC regularly, read books and journal articles on technology and telecommunications, and often use and encourage others to use ICONnect. These resources will extend the skills of library media specialists at all levels of technology proficiency so that they can teach others to be effective users and integrate technology into their program.

Some Final Thoughts

At the beginning of this section on Technology, Teachers, and the Library Media Specialist, an example related the disparity in student achievement between those whose teachers received technology training and those who did not—a rationale for why the library media specialist should assume the role of teacher of teachers. Further rationale follows. As critical as technology is to the achievement of students in school and as adults, in 1998 only 15 states had technology-related requirements for preservice teachers in order to receive their initial teaching credentials; 7 states were developing such requirements; 26 states had no plans to develop such requirements; and no data were available for 2 states. Additionally, just 4 states had technology-related continuing education requirements for teachers to maintain teaching credentials. Only 3 states had technology-related requirements for administrators in order to receive their initial credentials. Someone must assume leadership and ensure the academic achievement of students (Milken Exchange, 1998, 1–2). Visit Milken on the Web at <http://206.117.127.97/statepolicy/compcharts.taf?chart=3> and <http://www.milkenexchange.org/policy/statepolicy.html>.

In a paper entitled "Emerging Technologies: Applications and Implications for School Library Media Centers" (1994), Kathleen W. Craver gives advice to all school administrators and library media specialists:

In an increasingly competitive global economy, it will border on negligence if SLMCs [School Library Media Centers] fail to provide electronic information technologies. With improvements in telecommunications, access to multitype networks, declining costs in computers, and the availability of fax machines, school media specialists in even the smallest SLMCs should be able to provide users with some form of expanded access and document delivery.

Never before have SLMCs been so essential to their parent institutions. Our media center programs and service are educationally imperative if schools are to supply students with the skills, training and knowledge they must have to prosper in an electronic world environment. (Craver, 1994, 14, 15)

It is our responsibility to advocate for our program and help school officials understand the importance of technology to the instructional program of students today and its benefits to students as they become part of the work force in this country tomorrow.

In the words of President William Jefferson Clinton, "Technological literacy must become the standard in our country. Preparing children for a lifetime of computer use is just as essential today as teaching them the basics of reading, writing, and arithmetic" (Clinton, 1995, 1).

The next three sections of this chapter describe concepts and strategies that are especially supportive of the library media specialist as a curriculum partner.

Interdisciplinary Curriculum

In real-life situations, when we are confronted with a problem we gather data and derive solutions. We deal with the data in a holistic manner and not as individual pieces. The school day, which consists of 40- or 45-minute subject-specific classes, does not prepare students for this reality. Thus there is renewed interest in and recognition for an interdisciplinary curriculum (Jacobs, 1989, 1).

There are several reasons for this interest. First, knowledge is growing at an exponential rate. As a result, each subject field must figure out how to manage this new knowledge. Further, each year there are more topics to be included in the curriculum. Second, trying to fit content into prescribed periods fragments the day. Teachers complain that they have too much content to cover and not enough extended time with students. Students feel this fragmentation also. Third, the relevancy of the curriculum is an issue. Each day, students move from one subject to the other solving problems about each subject in isolation. Although it is important to help students see how specific subjects impact their lives, it is critical that they understand how the subjects are interconnected as well. Fourth, it is becoming evident that people cannot be trained in a specialization and then expected to work in a job where they are called on to perform a variety of skills. An interdisciplinary curriculum addresses all these issues (Jacobs, 1989, 3–6).

However, two problems that have been found in many interdisciplinary programs must be resolved. First, an interdisciplinary unit often includes just a sampling of information from each subject area. For example, if the subject is the Revolutionary War, there may be some information on the history, literature, the arts, and so forth, but often the unit lacks focus. The second problem, which is related to the first, has to do with the lack of clarity in curriculum design. This can result in anxiety among teachers who feel threatened when other teachers suggest changes to their curriculum. There is a need for both discipline-specific and interdisciplinary projects, units, and courses. In order to avert these two problems, carefully designed interdisciplinary curricula with a scope and sequence must be introduced. This should include a research process that promotes critical thinking and problem solving as well as a carefully designed assessment model that actively involves the student in learning (Jacobs, 1989, 2).

Interdisciplinary curriculum is increasingly being used, especially in elementary education. Our role as curriculum partner is especially critical as a member of the team creating an interdisciplinary unit or project. It is often in the library media center where the interdisciplinary team can find the focus for the unit, decide what they want students to be able to do at the end of the unit, determine a variety of acceptable assessments, and plan the learning activities as well as the instruction (Wiggins & McTighe, 1998, 9–13). The unit is most often dependent on resources that the library media center has available (including technology) or can acquire through interlibrary loan. Having access to necessary resources is critical to the success of the project. The evaluation of the unit also includes an assessment of the resources available to support the unit. In partnership with classroom teachers, we must collaborate on future purchases to provide necessary resources to support the unit.

Joan Enders, library media specialist at Monticello Middle School (with an enrollment of 900 students) in Longview, Washington, describes an endeavor that joins a unique technology program with an interdisciplinary unit. The unit was developed as part of a special program entitled "The Learning Space."

The Learning Space is a program collaboratively planned by numerous organizations in Washington State. The goal of the program is "to improve student learning by empowering educators across the state to use technology effectively in K–12 learning experiences." In 1996, there were 70 teachers in Washington State who were chosen as recipients of a US West/NEA Teacher Network Grant to initiate the program. The following year it was expanded to include 500 additional teachers, and I was one of these teachers. We were expected to spread the program by mentoring one new teacher the first year and then nine new teachers the second year. The program grew exponentially, thus greatly increasing the numbers of teachers using technology in their instructional plans. There were two types of programs teachers could develop: a global project or an online research investigation.

Our project, entitled "The 'Inside Story' On Desserts," is an example of a global project involving students in Puntas Arenas, Chile, South America. I collaborated with two sixth grade Health and Physical Education teachers from Monticello on this interdisciplinary project. We dovetailed a nutrition unit with a publishing project of the students' favorite desserts. The students' goal was to share their recipes with students outside the United States, in a culturally different area of the world. The students compared and contrasted the nutritional value of desserts enjoyed by themselves with those enjoyed by students in Chile, using electronic mail to communicate with their counterparts. The students found this part of the project very motivating. In addition, students compiled a cookbook that they gave to their mothers for Christmas. Chilean desserts were included.

This was a very technologically rich assignment. To illustrate, students entered their recipes onto a pre-formatted database form; compared types of desserts between the two communities by using a double bar graph; analyzed the desserts from both countries and made a pie chart of various nutritional values; and, finally, drew conclusions about desserts and nutrition from what they learned from the unit and what they saw in their results. They learned how to use a database entry; spreadsheets; pie charts; double bar graph charts; the Cut and Paste functions to insert information into a word processing document; and the insertion of graphics into a recipe.

Several of the Essential Academic Learning Requirements (EALRs), or state standards, addressed through this unit were drawn from the areas of Nutrition, Technology, and Reading. Examples of the EALRs follow: (1) Students will write effectively while entering recipes into the database; (2) Students will learn to analyze and evaluate what they eat, using the nutrition pyramid and generated spreadsheets; and (5) Students will be introduced to spreadsheet entry, chart making, database entry, email, and desktop publishing. Students were evaluated on every step of the project with a nutrition-styled rubric. This was a project that kept the students actively involved in their learning. The kids' responses to the unit were awesome. They learned to use technology effectively. (Joan Enders, personal communication, May 27, 1999)

Joan functioned as an instructional partner with the teachers in the planning, implementation, and assessment processes. This lesson may be viewed at Monticello Middle School's Web site at <http://www. teleport.com/~dewey/text/online.html>.

Cooperative Learning

A strategy that is becoming more commonly accepted by teachers and that supports the philosophy of the library media center as an extension of the classroom is cooperative learning. In all classrooms and in all subject areas as well as at all grade levels, teachers generally structure the instructional program to provide three types of experiences for students: working in small groups, independently, and in competition with their peers. An effective teacher designs learning experiences to incorporate all three methodologies for specific situations. Knowing how and when to structure the program to use these tools is a skill all teachers must develop (Johnson & Johnson, 1987, 1).

Cooperative learning groups, one type of small-group structure, constitute both an instructional as well as a social classroom framework to involve students in learning. It is a structure whereby the classroom teacher designs learning experiences in which there is positive interdependence, every member of the group has a task to accomplish and a role to fulfill, each member of the group contributes and is held accountable, and groups create a product and then present it to their classmates. In these heterogeneous groups, students share leadership as well as responsibility for each other, and social skills are taught by the teacher. While the teacher observes and intercedes when necessary by offering feedback on how well group members are working toward their objective or group task, the teacher structures the learning experience so that students can assess how well they are working together as a group (Johnson & Johnson, 1987, 14).

Johnson and Johnson suggest that, ideally, a cooperative group structure may be used for 60 to 70 percent of classroom time; an individualistic, 20 percent; and a competitive, 10 to 20 percent of the time (18).

Both task skills and group maintenance skills should be taught. Examples of task skills are "sharing information," "keeping the group on task," and "paraphrasing, elaborating, summarizing, testing and other ways of clarifying information." Examples of group maintenance skills are "checking for agreement," "sharing feelings," "gatekeeping," and "mediating" (Farmer, 1991, 4). It is also critical that the task of the group be clearly defined and explained by the teacher as well as understood by the students so they can productively work toward their goal rather than trying to interpret the assignment. A rubric, written directions, worksheets, or checklists that guide students through the process should be provided to each group. The process of cooperative learning, as well as the product and presentation, must be assessed by both the teacher and the students. The information can then be used by both parties to improve the next cooperative learning experience.

It takes time and experience for students to build relationships and develop trust with peers before they can share ideas and effectively produce a "real" group project (Johnson & Johnson, 1987, xii). This type of classroom or library media structure is similar to the type of structure students will encounter in the workplace.

Our role in cooperative learning is one of facilitator and curriculum partner with the classroom teacher in the design, implementation, and assessment of curricular projects. Cooperative learning groups spend much of their time in exploration, location, evaluation, and use of information. Often, one or two groups come to the media center while the other groups work in the classroom. Groups rotate regularly between the two work areas. While students are in the media center, we provide assistance with the information search process as well as information literacy standards, facilitating, guiding, and providing feedback as students complete their tasks. Finally, in collaboration with the teaching staff we must develop a library media collection that is rich in print and technology resources to respond to the needs and interests of students.

Karen S. Berdysiak, a sixth grade teacher at Clarence Middle School (with an enrollment of 1,000 students) in Clarence, New York, describes a cooperative learning experience in which she and Michelle McGhee, library media specialist, facilitate the group task:

I use cooperative learning groups throughout the school year. Students learn task skills as well as group maintenance skills at the beginning of the year, and these are reinforced at the start of each cooperative learning experience. Each student assumes a maintenance role within the group such as gatekeeper or clarifier as well as roles specific to the task. One of the cooperative as well as authentic learning experiences we completed this year was on political cartooning. Michelle and I collaborated during the planning stage to decide on activities in which students would participate as well as to create a rubric that included both the cooperative process and the students' product and presentation. When introducing the project and delineating the groups, I shared written instructions and several worksheets. In addition to the management roles, there were two task roles: "Connector," who was to facilitate brainstorming and assign tasks; and "Researcher," who was to locate information and take notes. There were two Researchers in each group who were assisted in their task by the worksheets.

The task for each cooperative group of three was to create a political cartoon to present to the class as a final product. One of the first activities planned was a visit to the library media center, where Michelle reviewed newspaper vocabulary that the students had learned in a previous unit in their language arts class. Students brainstormed the differences between fact and opinion related to news articles and editorials. Using a computer and LCD projector with an overhead projector and transparencies, Michelle showed several editorial cartoons and asked students to try to interpret them. She also explained two of the activities that would take place in the library media center and introduced available resources. Student questions were answered so that they were clear about their task.

There were three distinct activities in this project. Activity One took place in the library media center and in the classroom. Each group had to locate a political cartoon dealing with an event in history. The group had to then research background information about the event or situation that was being depicted. Finally, they had to make a transparency of the cartoon, share it with their classmates, and communicate their research concerning the event or situation depicted in the cartoon. For example, one historical cartoon was concerned with one of Theodore Roosevelt's presidential election campaigns. Students had to locate information on the candidates and issues, and on the Bullmoose Party.

Activity Two also took place in the library media center and the classroom. Each group had to locate current political cartoons from the *Buffalo News; USA Today;* or *Time* magazine and follow the same procedure for research and presentation as for Activity One. Activity Three took place in the classroom. The task roles for this activity changed. There were a "Connector," who was to graphically organize, brainstorm the ideas of the group, and keep members organized; an "Illustrator," who was to draw the cartoon related to the issue; and a "Literary Enricher," who was to create a catchy phrase that summed up the illustrator's picture. One of the following topics was assigned to each group: "A man was denied rental of an apartment because he has children." "A woman complains that her neighbor constantly plays loud music." "A family wants additional garbage pick-up days in their neighborhood because they have a lot of garbage." "A man thinks he was not given a job in the town library because of his age. He is 63 years old." Students had to create cartoons in their groups, with each student having a different task role. In the end, each group presented its cartoon to the class. The class was asked to guess the issue to determine if the cartoon got its point across.

In this cooperative project, students assumed at least two different maintenance and task roles, made group decisions, had individual assignments upon which the success of their group depended, shared the leadership at different times, had several presentations where they taught their subject or cartoon to the rest of the class, created three separate products, and participated in a process that involved them in their learning. There was positive interdependence demonstrated in these groups. Students received the rubric at the beginning of the project, which they used to participate in their assessment of both the cooperative process and the cartoons.

Cooperative learning is very important because it helps students learn from their peers and be able to see value to what they have to offer. Cooperative learning helps to engage all students and highlights their talents. There are a variety of roles associated with cooperative learning, and this helps every student fit in and feel comfortable with the learning process. (Karen S. Berdysiak, personal communication, June 10, 1999)

The Learning Pyramid distributed by the National Training Laboratories in Bethel, Maine (n.d.), strengthens the need for students to work in cooperative groups. The Pyramid graphically shows the average retention rate for types of learning activities. The average retention rate for a lecture is just 5 percent; for reading, 10 percent; for audiovisual materials, 20 percent; for a demonstration, 30 percent; for a discussion group, 50 percent; for practice by doing, 75 percent; and for teaching others, making immediate use of learning, 90 percent! This is critical information for both ourselves as media specialists and the classroom teacher as we design learning activities for students. We must provide opportunities to make immediate use of learning by teaching others. Co-operative learning is an excellent vehicle to accomplish this.

Learning Styles

For library media specialists and classroom teachers to assist all students in their instructional program, they must understand the learning styles of each individual. The range of student learning styles influences the methodology a teacher uses and requires certain types of resources to be available in the library media center. Howard Gardner discusses multiple intelligences in *Frames of Mind* (1983), in which he identifies seven intelligences. The traditional view of intelligence acknowledged only two intelligences, verbal (language) and computational (mathematical). The seven intelligences defined by Gardner are:

- Linguistic Intelligence, the ability to effectively use language in writing, speaking, and listening.
- Logical-Mathematical Intelligence, the ability to use inductive and deductive reasoning to solve abstract problems and to use numbers effectively.
- Spatial Intelligence, the ability to perceive the visual-spatial world accurately; be able to visualize, create mental models, and represent visual or spatial ideas to solve problems.
- Musical Intelligence, the ability to recognize musical elements and compose with musical pitches, tones, and rhythms.
- Bodily-Kinesthetic Intelligence, the ability to use mental proficiency to coordinate bodily movements, establishing harmony between mind and body.
- Interpersonal Intelligence, the ability to understand and be able to work with other people.
- Intrapersonal Intelligence, the ability to understand one's own feelings and motivations and use this information to operate effectively in life. (Armstrong, 1994, 2, 3; Brualdi, 1998, 26; Gardner, 1983, 73–276; Parry, 1999, 12).

Although individuals possess all seven intelligences, each person has unique strengths and weaknesses. This set of intelligences determines how easy or difficult it is for an individual to learn when information is presented in a particular manner. Gardner asserts that the intelligences generally operate in concern with one another as individuals solve problems (Brualdi, 1998, 26).

The theory maintains that all seven intelligences are necessary for individuals to function successfully. Therefore, teachers should consider each intelligence of equal importance, constructing lessons and units to include most or all of the intelligences. Collaboration with the library media specialist at the planning stage will lead to the design of activities that make use of a broad range of resources providing depth of topics for both teacher and students while addressing different intelligences. For example, when studying the Civil War, through maps of the period students can learn where battles took place (Spatial); through music of the period students can learn songs that were sung by soldiers (Musical); through literature students can read about life during the period (Linguistic); by developing a timeline of battles students can practice logical thinking (Logical-Mathematical); by constructing dioramas students can depict specific events of the war (Body-Kinesthetic); through cooperative learning groups and the use of logs and journals, students can expand their ability to understand themselves as well as others (Interpersonal and Intrapersonal.) This type of lesson not only engages students as they learn about the Civil War through various learning styles but also provides a deeper understanding of the topic (Brualdi, 1998, 27).

It would be impossible to teach every lesson using all seven intelligences, but the teacher can help students use their more highly developed intelligences to understand subject matter in the areas of less developed intelligences. For instance, a student who has a keen musical intelligence may compose music or a rap song to demonstrate understanding about a theorem in geometry. By identifying the intelligences of each student, the teacher and library media specialist can design appropriate learning activities and assessment models (Brualdi, 1998, 28).

Following are suggestions for student activities that utilize the respective intelligence (Parry, 1999, 13):

Linguistic: oral reports/sharing, speeches, debates

Logical-Mathematical: logic puzzles, timelines, experimentation

Spatial: graphic organizers, pattern blocks, models

Musical: instrumental, choral reading, singing

Bodily-Kinesthetic: dance, construction, sports

Interpersonal: cooperative grouping, role play, tutors/buddies

Intrapersonal: metacognition, logs/journals, goal setting

By attending to students' strengths and helping them develop additional areas of intelligence, we ensure that students will gain a greater ability to solve problems. Awareness of the types of intelligences enables us to function as facilitator and partner with the teacher as students work on collaboratively planned activities, projects, and units to master information literacy standards. Additionally, we must provide a broadly based and in-depth collection of resources to engage students in their strengths as they are actively involved in their learning.

Effective implementation of the library media program is dependent on many variables. Where the program is collaboratively planned by teachers and the library media specialist, flexible scheduling is in place, resource-based learning is used, library media specialist and teachers model a research process for interdisciplinary units and other information search assignments, technology is utilized as a teaching and learning tool, students cooperate in groups to model their future work experience, and the instructional program meets the learning styles of students to improve their academic achievement, the library media program as well as the instructional program will have responded to the call for educational reform in the schools. Students will be information-literate adults.

ASSESSMENT

Assessment is the last step in the instructional design model and the one in which library media specialists have had the least experience. Implementation and assessment of the instructional program are seamless. Teachers and the library media specialist plan a unit to actively involve students in their learning by deciding what they want students to be able to do at the end of the unit, designing a variety of appropriate assessments to engage them in the process, and planning the learning activities that provide students with meaningful choices. Students plan their learning, produce a product, present their learning to others, and, finally, participate in self-assessment of both the process they used and the product and presentation they developed, thereby demonstrating their ability to be independent learners. They learn valuable information by reflecting on these aspects of the instructional unit as well. Teachers and the library media specialist assess the process, product, and presentation and share results with students. This scenario describes the type of assessment in which some library media specialists are presently participating, and in which others will participate as educational reform moves forward.

This section provides an overview of the assessment process that will help library media specialists understand current theory, models, and practice. This information is needed in order to function as a curriculum partner in the assessment process.

Although the terms *assessment* and *evaluation* are often used interchangeably, there is a significant difference. Regie Routman (1994) suggests that "assessment" pertains to the collection of data or the gathering of information but that "evaluation" is the "interpretation, analysis, and reflection" that brings meaning to that data. Whereas "evaluation" is dependent on "assessment," "assessment" is only the beginning of the "evaluation" process (302). Heidi Hayes Jacobs (1997) defines assessment as a demonstration of student learning—evidence that they learned skills as well as process, acquired knowledge, understood concepts, and either grew or regressed in their learning and process (11).

Purpose of Assessment

The purpose of assessment is to help students and teachers constantly improve (Wiggins, 1997, 2). This is accomplished by providing information to the student as well as the teacher and library media specialist. In terms of the student, monitoring progress and providing feedback throughout the unit prompt students to learn and adjust their learning accordingly, thereby promoting growth. In addition, recognizing student achievement at the end of the unit enables students to understand how well they performed in relation to the expectations. In terms of the teacher and library media specialist, ongoing feedback and assessment enable the partners to improve instruction by modifying the instructional design. Evaluating the overall program leads to other modifications as well (Donham, 1998, 7, 8).

Assessment is very different from the traditional form of evaluation that takes place at the end of a project with little feedback to students other than a final grade. Generally, in the traditional approach the teacher does not gather data from students during a unit that would indicate the need to alter instruction. Students are unsure that what they are learning is germane to the unit and do not find this out until the grade has been assigned. As a result of test scores, the teacher may or may not modify the unit for the next time the project is presented.

Standardized Testing

Standardized tests are forms of evaluation, not assessment. However, they must be discussed in juxtaposition to assessment. In fact, it is because of standardized tests that alternative types of assessment have been devised. Much has been written about bias in standardized tests—racial, ethnic, gender, and socioeconomic—as well as the resultant placement of students. Yet standardized testing has become regulated in our nation's schools—an accepted annual practice. Delia Neuman, quoting Neill and Medina (1989) reports that during the 1986–1987 school year 105 million standardized tests were administered to 39.8 million students and that by the time a student graduates from high school he or she may have taken 30 standardized tests. Further exacerbating this situation, many teacher-made tests model the standardized test format of multiple choice. Although there is an acknowledgment that standardized tests have become "better" in recent years, there is a growing movement to shift to an alternative type of test that would better evaluate student abilities and achievement (Neuman, 1994, 67–69).

Although much has been written describing the problems related to standardized testing, they are an excellent method for recognizing student accomplishment. In addition, an item analysis of standardized test results can identify areas in the curriculum that need to be modified or changed to address the needs of students (Donham, 1998, 23). If used for these purposes, standardized testing can provide valuable information to the teacher and district administrators.

Even though the use of standardized and other traditional tests such as multiple choice will probably continue, a growing number of people and groups support alternative assessment.

Alternative Assessment

Alternative assessment is a relatively new concept in education. It began to appear in elementary and secondary education literature and practice between the mid and late 1980s. Several states are presently using an alternative assessment model. California, Connecticut, Kentucky, New York, Rhode Island, and Vermont are leaders in this movement (Neuman, 1994, 70).

Regardless of the form of alternative assessment, the concept has some common elements:

- Assessment is embedded in the learning process—assessment and curriculum become one.

- There is an emphasis on the learning process, not just on the product. Students are actively constructing meaning throughout the process (Herman, Aschbacher, & Winters, 1992, 13).

- Students are at the center of their learning and receive continuous feedback. When they "actively" make connections between their prior knowledge and information need, they construct new knowledge based on existing information rather than "inactively" hearing and reading information presented by others (Neuman, 1994, 69).

- Genuine student products are assessed such as essays, demonstrations, computer simulations, exhibits, and similar displays. This replaces the indirect method provided by tests (Neuman, 1994, 69).

In alternative assessment, students use problem-solving and higher order thinking skills, ultimately taking responsibility for their learning. Throughout this process the library media specialist facilitates students' learning as they work toward constructing a final product (Neuman 1994, 72–73).

Some educators and researchers have cautioned about the inadequacy of teacher training in assessment models, the amount of time it takes to implement a program, and the lack of common assessments of materials students create (Neuman, 1994, 71–72). Although these concerns persist, alternative assessment continues to gain momentum. Let's look at several types of alternative assessments.

Authentic Assessment

Although authentic assessment is an alternative method of gauging student achievement, not all alternative assessment is authentic. Authentic assessment is based on authentic, or real-life, learning experiences. It measures student performance throughout the experience and is based on important concepts determined by the teacher. These are consistent with accepted district curricula and build on prior information and knowledge that require a high level of thinking from students (Peters [1991], quoted in Stripling, 1994a, 79). Reflection, also, is a critical element in authentic assessment. Students must reflect on the process and product to assess their strengths and areas of need so they can integrate this information into the next real-life learning experience and improve the process. Teachers must reflect on the process to evaluate the relevance of the type of assessment used for the content presented as well as the activities and strategies selected (Stripling, 1994a, 80). Students make connections between what they know (prior knowledge) and what they are learning, in an effort to construct new knowledge. They are engaged in meaningful inquiry as they construct this new knowledge through real-life, authentic learning and assessment activities.

The library media specialist's role in authentic assessment is one of facilitator, for both the student and the classroom teacher. We facilitate learning for both groups when we collaborate on learning experiences, provide resources to support them, and work to match resources to students' abilities and interests within the structure of the instructional unit. We also facilitate authentic assessment when we help students access, evaluate, and use information in preparation for a presentation that will be part of the assessment. Additionally, in partnership with the classroom teacher assisting students to reflect on the process and the product, we facilitate learning as a participant in the assessment of the authentic activity.

Alternative and Authentic Testing

Unlike the multiple choice test, alternative and authentic tests should measure significant content and not ancillary information; they should measure depth of a topic rather than its breadth. They should require students to think and apply their understandings and knowledge to situations rather than respond with a repetition of facts. These tests should provide an opportunity for students to demonstrate what they have learned. For the test to be authentic, it must include real-life situations (Stripling, 1994a, 81–82). This is essential information for both the classroom teacher and library media specialist as they create assessment tools.

Portfolios

Portfolios are a systematic collection of student work over time showing progress toward instructional objectives (Callison, 1998, 42). Students set goals and criteria for what will be included in the portfolio; these must be consistent with teacher goals and criteria as well as state or national learning standards. Because students periodically review their work and make reflective decisions about what will be included in the portfolio, they are at the center of the assessment process and are practicing critical thinking skills that help them become independent learners. During this formative period, through writing students are responsible for explaining how the pieces they include meet their goals or standards and demonstrate learning that has been acquired (Stripling, 1994a, 82–83). The portfolio is used as a summative tool as well, exhibiting the growth and accomplishments of the student (Donham, 1998, 23).

As a compilation of performance tasks, the portfolio demonstrates mastery or achievement of the student's goals. It shows a student's progress over time. Many types of items can be included in a portfolio: written reports, writing samples, notes from an oral or written report, drafts showing the stages of development of a product, learning logs and journals, reflective and creative pieces, videotapes and cassettes, art work, Hypercard stacks, graphic organizers, charts, timelines, data sheets, homework, rubrics, a list of reference tools used in research, and exhibits of products created as a result of student learning (Angle et al., 1997, 10; Stripling, 1994a, 82–83).

The library media specialist's role in portfolio assessment is one of facilitator as both the classroom teacher and specialist guide students in developing information literacy and gathering specimens for the portfolio. Furthermore, students must have the opportunity to reflect on the information literacy standards and how their skills improved as a result of the assignment. This should be done after the product is complete. This type of self-assessment should also be included in the student's portfolio to provide evidence of growth or progression through the levels of information literacy standards (Callison, 1994, 128).

Performances

Although performances in areas such as communication, music, and foreign language have traditionally demonstrated students' level of learning, there are many other curriculum areas where performance-based assessment may be used as well. Fourth grade students may demonstrate an electricity experiment, seventh grade students may re-enact a historical event in their state that they have researched, or eleventh grade students may debate a social issue, (e.g., lengthening the school year or legalizing drugs) after analyzing the pros and cons of that issue. The performance may be presented individually or in small groups before the class or to larger groups (Stripling, 1994a, 84–85).

Performance-based assessment has many advantages. For students to present a performance, they must develop a greater understanding of the issues and concepts than a mere reading or perusal of the content would provide. Students gain greater self-esteem as well. Performances are often developed by a group of students, and the teacher and library media specialist act as facilitators (Stripling, 1994a, 84–85). Performance takes many forms: *Oral*—speech, report, proposal, debate, simulation, discussion; *Written*—essay, letter, report, script, proposal, poem or song, log, memoir; *Display*—exhibit, constructed model, graph/chart/table, electronic media, advertisement, artistic visual medium, demonstration (Katims, 1999, 8). This is not an exhaustive list; it is meant to inspire thinking.

However, there are limitations. Because a performance generally takes place at the end of the unit or activity, it must be accompanied by other types of assessment tools such as a rubric or checklist. Further, it takes much more class time to complete than either tests or portfolios, especially if all students choose to do a performance. In addition, it is difficult to evaluate. Teachers should not evaluate the performances of their own students because it is difficult to be objective. Performances should be rated on a scale that reflects how well students perform in relation to a standard or goal; they should not be compared to other students. Finally, it is difficult to assess the individual student when she or he is a member of a group. While teachers struggle with these issues, performance assessments continue to be included in instructional units (Stripling, 1994a, 85).

The library media specialist's role is invaluable to teachers through various levels of program development—from planning the assessment collaboratively with the teacher as part of the project; to providing feedback and guidance to students in the research and writing processes; to including technology in accessing information as well as in the production of presentations; to serving as an evaluator of the presentations; to creating a section in the professional library that addresses different assessment models; to sharing professional books and journal articles, on a regular basis, with teachers, principal, and interested members of the learning community. Finally, we can become expert in assessment and provide informal as well as formal staff development on this topic, or we can arrange workshops in which teachers work together on assessment methodology.

Assessment Tools

Feedback is essential to students' learning. Normally, students do not understand or learn concepts the first time they are presented. They learn from nonjudgmental feedback they receive from their teacher and library media specialist. Feedback is descriptive, not evaluative: it is a description of what the student did or did not do, a description of the student's performance or product. It is not praise or blame, nor is it guidance. Rather than being told what to do, students decide what they need to do next or differently—part of the process whereby they are actively involved in their learning (Wiggins, 1997, 3–6). Although feedback can take many forms, the more frequently used tools follow.

Rubrics

Historically teachers have assigned a grade, 0–100, to show the quality of student work. However, if the same work was given to five different teachers, there may have been five different grades. The use of a rubric gives students and parents an in-depth explanation of value. A rubric is a scale for scoring an activity, project, or unit that addresses specific goals and describes the performance at different levels of competency. A rubric is designed to help students locate themselves on a continuum and provide direction so they can move to the next level. It describes success, gives students feedback throughout the learning process, and helps to assess student work objectively. It is commonly used for assessing performance and portfolios.

A clearly defined goal is primary to developing a rubric. However, as a unit is created, the goal may change. Because the trait or scoring criterion is a direct outgrowth of the goal or purpose, it is important to periodically check the rubric against the goal to keep them parallel. Included in a rubric are: one or more traits; a scale for levels of achievement, such as 1 = basic, 2 = proficient, and 3 = advanced (Callison, 1998, 43); and standards of excellence, or descriptors, for performance levels defining "basic" or "advanced" level as well as "needs improvement" or "quality work." Examples are supplied that describe different levels of achievement as well (Chicago Board of Education, 1999, 1). Visit <http://intranet.cps.k12.il.us/Assessments/Ideas_and_Rubrics/ideas_and_rubrics.html>. For more information about rubrics and assessment, visit Kathy Schrock's Web site (1999): <http://discoveryschool.com/schrockguide/assess.html>. Kathy Schrock is technology coordinator, Dennis-Yarmouth Regional School District in Yarmouth, Massachusetts.

Rubrics are presented to students along with the project so that they know, before they begin, the criteria or expectations on which their work will be judged. In this way, they can work on solving the problem rather than wondering what the teacher expects. The student refers to the rubric often during the project or task. Rubrics also promote learning by providing clear performance targets for levels of competence for student learning. If students choose a higher level of achievement, they will gain additional learning. The contrary is true as well (Donham, 1998, 8–10).

Because rubrics can be time consuming to construct, it is helpful to locate basic rubrics that have been developed by different states, organizations, authors, and school districts. These can be adapted as specific activities and tasks to assess students' achievement are created.

Following are the first, third, and fifth (last) levels of the overview and framework for the Information Literacy Rubrics for School Library Media Specialists, State Library and Adult Education Office and the Colorado Educational Media Association, quoted from *From Library Skills to Information Literacy: A Handbook for the 21st Century* (1997) by the California School Library Association (CSLA). The reader will be able to see the progression of quality as well as the traits, levels of achievement, and standards of excellence or descriptors for specified performance levels in this rubric.

Student as a Knowledge Seeker (first level)

> In Progress—I need someone to tell me when I need information, what information I need, and help me find it.

> Essential—Sometimes I can identify my information needs. I ask for help finding and using information.

> Proficient—I am able to determine when I have a need for information.

> Advanced—I know my information needs. I am confident that I can solve problems by selecting and processing information.

Student as a Self-Directed Learner (third level)

> In Progress— I have trouble choosing my own resources and I like someone to tell me the answer.

> Essential—I might know what I want, but need to ask for help in solving information problems.

> Proficient—I choose my own resources and like being independent in my information searches.

> Advanced—I like to choose my own information resources. I am comfortable in situations where there are multiple answers as well as those with no answers.

Student as a Responsible Information User (fifth level)

> In Progress—If I find information I can use, I copy it directly. I need to be reminded about being polite and about sharing resources and equipment with others.

> Essential—I usually remember to give credit when I use someone else's ideas. It is okay for others to have different ideas from mine. I try to be polite and share information resources and equipment with others.

> Proficient—I do not plagiarize. I understand the concept of intellectual freedom. I am polite and share resources and equipment with others.

> Advanced—I follow copyright laws and guidelines. I help others understand the concept of intellectual freedom, and can defend my rights if challenged. I acknowledge and respect the rights of others to use information resources and equipment (CSLA, 1997, 135).

If a project is designed to measure three information literacy standards, there must be three sets of rubrics. If a rubric is appropriate for another activity, project, or unit, it may be used again. This helps students assess their growth and reach increasingly competent levels of performance (Donham, 1998, 10).

A rubric is not an appropriate assessment technique for all information processing tasks. For example, if a student is asked to write a bibliographic citation or locate a title in the online public access catalog, he or she can do the task correctly or not. In this situation a rubric is not suitable. However, if a student is asked to create a short paper on one of the battles of the Civil War and there is a continuum of developing quality, a rubric is an excellent technique to assess the product, helping the student understand what is expected through a clear explanation of the grading system (Donham, 1998, 10).

Journals

During a project students are accessing, evaluating, and using information. Keeping a journal or log can provide the teacher, library media specialist, and students with insight into both the process and the product. As students reflect on and write about their learning by responding to specific questions, they focus on important knowledge and accomplishments: when they felt successful as well as when they experienced stress and anxiety; where their information literacy problems occurred; how they solved them; which problems remained to be solved; and what still needs to be accomplished. These brief statements show the teacher and library media specialist where the student is in the research process and indicate where additional instruction is necessary. Journals can play an important role in the learning process if students review them as they begin work on their next research project (Donham, 1998, 9). These tools help students stay focused or recognize the need to seek assistance from the teacher or library media specialist. Teachers and library media specialists can also maintain a journal or log including observations of classes or individuals, a specific behavior, or group dynamics within a class. The student, teacher, and library media specialist record what happened and how they felt but do not include personal judgment. Journals and logs can help the teacher and library media specialist better understand the students and can help the students better understand their own skills, attitudes, learnings, and understandings (Stripling, 1994a, 86; Stripling, 1994b, 108–109).

Checklists

Checklists are designed to guide students through a project or unit. They identify points in the research process at which students must get approval from the teacher or library media specialist before moving on.

Like a rubric, a checklist should be presented at the beginning of the project. The criteria should be clear: for example, Topic Accepted; Research Question Accepted; Notes Organized; and so forth. There should also be a place for the teacher or library media specialist to give feedback, indicate dates when items must be complete, and write his or her initials once the project is complete (Donham, 1998, 12, 13).

Other Tools

Conferences with students as well as observations of their process will provide additional opportunities to provide feedback, which is essential to student learning.

CONCLUSION

The classroom teacher and library media specialist must select assessment processes and techniques that are most applicable to a given project and group of students. The measures chosen should provide the teacher and library media specialist with the most information about students and their information processing skills and give students the best guidance.

Student assessment is based on learning experiences. Assessing student progress toward a finished product is continuous. Because the teacher wants the largest number of assessments in order to gain the broadest and most definitive perspective of student performance, the teacher may include several processes. Teaching and learning are embedded in the assessment process. Library media specialists must become proficient at designing and using assessment instruments, helping classroom teachers define the criteria for information literacy standards, and collaborating with them on the assessment of student performance. In your roles as curriculum partners, you and the classroom teachers will make significant contributions to redefining the instructional program for students.

Staff Development: Redefining Opportunities for Learning

7

Staff development is key to becoming a leader who can effect change. If the changes described in the library media profession are to come to fruition, library media specialists must pursue their own professional development as well as provide teachers and administrators with professional development programs.

Staff development, professional development, continuing education, or in-service—terms that are used interchangeably—is a composite of the continuing educational experiences, both formal and informal, throughout one's career (Fullan, 1991, 326). These experiences can take the form of college courses, seminars, and distance learning courses as well as school district programs. The last category represents the largest form of staff development presented today and has the greatest potential for success (316).

The role of library media specialist in staff development is twofold: as both a student or participant in staff development, and as a teacher or facilitator of staff development for others. We must appreciate the opportunities to learn and place a high value on professional growth so that we not only are students of formal staff development but are actively assimilating appropriate practices into the library media program, creating our own methods and strategies as well as expanding and stretching our roles as library media specialist and teacher leader (Hug, 1988, 116).

Although there are many benefits to the individual participant of staff development, the organization benefits also. There is increased faculty morale; leadership emerges from among the staff; people feel an ownership of and commitment to the school's programs; the learning community environment is improved; and lines of communication are opened throughout the school.

Senge (1990) describes the learning community as constituting people learning to learn together, thinking together, sharing ideas, and developing visions that are shared by others (6–10). Carefully constructed staff development can build this type of learning community.

LIBRARY MEDIA SPECIALIST
AS STUDENT OF STAFF DEVELOPMENT

It is vital for library media specialists to be students of staff development because of the magnitude of change that commands our attention— educational, social, economic, and technological. We cannot expect that what we learn during the formal educational process before entering the work force will provide us with the knowledge and skills necessary to continue to function optimally and to teach others during this information-rich period. The changes in technology alone have revolutionized the library media profession, and we must become experts in this area.

Additionally, as students of instructional staff development we must not only understand concepts teachers are learning and integrating into their programs but implement them in our own programs as much as possible. For library media specialists to understand the challenges and be part of the teaching team in solving the problems of implementation and assessment, we must be a participant with them in the district's staff development program—a part of the process. We cannot learn about the concepts after the fact and then expect to be accepted as a partner. An increased sense of collegiality, cooperation, and belonging are important byproducts of this process.

Finally, we must have the knowledge and skill base necessary to be a teacher leader and to provide staff development for teachers in our building, within the school district or learning community, and at local, state, and national conferences. In these roles as change agent, we must understand adult learning principles and know what effective staff development is, so that we will be able to, in turn, plan and execute effective programming.

What Is Effective Staff Development?

Successful staff development depends on both the motivation of the individual and the learning opportunities that are available (Fullan, 1991, 326). In most learning communities today, there is a significant number of staff development opportunities. However, because motivation is intrinsic, it is the individual who must value the experience or feel that she will benefit from the involvement or that the learning will benefit her students. She must make a commitment to manage her own learning to improve the knowledge and skill base so that she can improve the level of instruction for students. If the characteristics of an effective staff development program are present, individuals will be motivated to participate.

The Change Process

Because change is the objective of staff development, planners must recognize and integrate the elements of the change process into the program, understand how people respond to a new idea, and address the stages through which they go before the change has been accepted and assimilated. Time should be provided at the outset to discuss the concerns of the participants regarding the change, rather than the concerns of the trainers (Loucks-Horsley et al., 1987, 15). The change process is discussed more fully in Chapter 3.

Adult Learning Principles

Adults learn differently from children. Therefore, specific conditions must be present. Adults learn best when they are voluntary participants in the process; have an investment in their self-improvement; and assume responsibility for their learning (Brookfield, 1986, 30; Loucks-Horsley et al., 1987, 11). Requiring people to participate in staff development will not be successful if they have not made a commitment to be involved. Does this mean that there is never mandatory staff development? On the contrary it means that both the process and content of the program must be structured to meet the needs of the adult learners so that they will choose to participate and be committed to learn.

Adults learn best when they are actively involved in their learning; when they collaborate in as many decision points as is possible (e.g., needs assessment, goal setting, planning, implementation, and evaluation); when they are participants in small group discussions, practice and feedback, coaching, cooperative learning, role playing, case studies, observations, buzz groups, and the like, rather than in lectures (Loucks-Horsley et al., 1987, 11, 14, 15). Connections between (1) the participants' experiences and needs, and (2) the presenters' content, must be extensive. We know that this is true of student learning as well. Teachers must provide many opportunities to involve students in their learning.

Finally, adult learners must have ample time to read and reflect on the concepts and skills being learned, receive support as they implement new practices, and have an opportunity to evaluate the best practices relative to the individual (Loucks-Horsley et al., 1987, 11). There is a cycle of learning: exploration and investigation; activity to test this learning;

time to reflect on the experience; and then further exploration and investigation, activity, and reflection (Brookfield, 1986, 15). The participant must view her classroom as a laboratory in which to experiment with new methods, take risks, adjust techniques, reflect, fail, and try again, all without penalty. She must feel support in failure as well as in success. She must also feel challenged, because it is through challenge that participants grow. This ongoing instruction, testing of ideas, support, and evaluation will help the participant to assimilate the change more readily.

- *The staff development program begins with the administration of a comprehensive needs assessment to determine the specific needs of the participants.* This is one of the decision points at which participants are involved in the process (Kearney, 1990, 54).
- *The staff development program is built on the philosophy and goals of the school or district.* It is an integral component of the school or district's development and structure, not something added on to the program as an unconnected project (Fullan, 1991, 331).
- *The school district supports the program.* Leadership from key administrators within the school and district, as well as the resources necessary to successfully implement a staff development program, are critical to an effective program (Darish, 1987, 329). These leaders legitimize and sustain the staff development effort (Loucks-Horsley et al., 1987, 13).
- *The program is part of a long-term, systematic, and comprehensive staff development program.* Its continuity and logic are coordinated to build on skills and concepts already learned, and it provides continual follow-through on these concepts. This allows people to resolve issues that might otherwise keep them from integrating the concept (Darish, 1987, 329–330).
- *Collegiality and cooperation are developed.* An effective program builds collegiality and cooperation among participants and reduces the isolation felt by many library media specialists. It enables participants to connect with other staff members, share challenges, solve problems, and provide assistance to one another. It presents the opportunity to network among peers, providing support as well as resources (Fullan, 1991, 330).
- *The program is conducted during the school day.* The most successful staff development programs are conducted during school time. This can be accomplished through the creative use of teacher planning time as well as the practice of staff members covering classes for their peers once collegiality and cooperation have been developed. In addition, programs can be conducted before school and during early dismissal or full days scheduled on the district's calendar when students are not in attendance (Fullan, 1991, 330). Not only is the staff more alert during the day, but if the principal arranges for classes to be covered, it sends a powerful message that he is committed to staff development.
- *Appropriate rewards and incentives are provided.* An effective program provides appropriate rewards and incentives (intrinsic as well as extrinsic) for partici-

pants. Although extrinsic rewards such as certificates, pay increases, and college credit are desirable, the intrinsic rewards are often more meaningful to participants; these are derived from sharing ideas and meeting with peers, gaining competence by increasing knowledge and skills, and achieving success (Kearney, 1990, 55). Professional growth is in itself a reward.

- *The quality of programming is maintained.* An effective program provides a site that is easily accessible and has been properly prepared as well as presenters who have been selected on the basis of their competence. Demonstrations by outstanding practitioners should also be an essential component of the staff development program (Darish, 1987, 329–330). Knowledge bases about teaching skills, student learning styles, integration of technology, and others should be incorporated into the program as needs are identified (Loucks-Horsley et al., 1987, 10).

- *The program is evaluated.* Effective staff development is continually evaluated and modified so that the needs of participants are met. The program should be evaluated in terms of its goals, objectives, and appropriateness for participants' knowledge, skills, and experiences (Darish, 1987, 329–330).

If these characteristics are a part of the district, school, and departmental staff development programs, participants will be volunteers and will accept responsibility for their learning.

LIBRARY MEDIA SPECIALIST AS
TEACHER LEADER OF STAFF DEVELOPMENT

The library media specialist has a unique opportunity to be a teacher leader of staff development. The very nature of our function in a school puts us in a position to assist and facilitate the learning of others—teachers, students, administrators, other staff, and parents. As a library media specialist and teacher leader, you will be called on to assist teachers and other members of the learning community in much the same manner as you assist students: at their point of need. This will be reflected in informal as well as formal staff development, and individual as well as small group and large group participation.

Informal Staff Development

Much of the staff development in which we are involved as teacher leader is informal. It happens one on one, every day of the school year. We talk with staff in the hallway, the lunch room, the lounge, or the library media center. Knowing the teachers and having established a working relationship with each one, we use our leadership skills to determine what knowledge and skills an individual needs. We must not wait until teachers come to us for assistance but must be proactive and search them out.

Informal staff development activities that we may perform for teachers include: informing them of journal articles, books, and instructional media that would be helpful to them; offering instruction on computer and audiovisual equipment or programs in the library media center and encouraging them to utilize these tools in their instructional program activities; sharing an outstanding program that has applications to other curricular areas; planning programs with them; suggesting resources for a particular unit; providing an orientation for new teachers on the library media center program, including services, programs, planning, and the integration of information literacy standards into the curriculum; and informing them about staff development courses offered by the district, teacher center, or state education department, distance learning opportunities, and local colleges and universities as well as state and national conferences (Watkins & Craft, 1988, 112).

There may be informal opportunities to provide staff development to small groups as well. For example, at all school levels there are people who are interested in different genres of literature. You might offer a summary of picture book authors, folk tales, or storytelling for the primary level teachers; a summary of biographies for middle school teachers; or authors for ninth grade Language Arts teachers including a demonstration of a book talk. A needs assessment can determine if there is an interest in specific topics.

Several years ago Barbara A. Hull, library media specialist at one of the elementary schools in the West Seneca Central School District, a suburban district in West Seneca, New York, developed a six-week program on folk tales as a result of many questions by teachers. She conducted a simple survey to determine interest, discussed the program with the principal, planned individual sessions, and sent a memo to teachers. As a result she conducted special 45-minute workshops for a six-week period with a group of eight staff members. In the month following the workshops, the folklore collection in her library media center was in constant circulation and was incorporated in the literature programs in at least eight classrooms (Barbara A. Hull, personal communication, May 19, 1999).

These informal opportunities to provide services develop a recognition of your expertise and willingness to assist teachers at their point of need; they also promote partnerships with teachers and staff.

Formal Staff Development

Library media specialists should be involved in formal staff development programs at both the school and district levels. Your expertise as an information specialist, teacher, and curriculum partner, as well as your leadership skills, make you an important member of the staff development team at both levels. If your school has a site-based decision-making team or leadership team, lobby to become a member if you are not already. It is here that decisions of all types impacting the formal and informal operation of the school take place. Perhaps your site-based or leadership team has a subcommittee that addresses staff development. As a member of this team and subcommittee, you can focus more attention on the library media program as a critical factor in restructuring instruction and improving student achievement.

As a teacher leader of staff development, you bring expertise and skills to the table, recommending issues such as information literacy and technology, which are challenges in all areas of the curriculum. In this role you must not only demonstrate leadership skills but also competence in group process skills such as building consensus, conflict resolution, group facilitation, problem solving, and decision making.

If your school does not have a committee addressing the needs of staff development, encourage your administrator to form such a committee and create a comprehensive plan. Volunteer to be a member of the committee and move the process toward an effective staff development program. In the words of Philip Turner, the library media specialist's role is to "help teachers teach" (1993). Through both informal and formal staff development, you will make strides toward the fulfillment of this role.

Finally, if your school or district has no staff development program in place, it is important that you create one for the library media program by assessing the needs of the staff.

Regardless of the level at which you enter the staff development process, you must be actively involved in providing information and training for teachers. Mary Alice Anderson, media specialist at Winona Middle School in Winona, Minnesota, is adamant.

Instead of complaining about the way things are, become a part of the solution and get involved in staff development. We are in a unique situation and can see the "big picture." We must correlate staff development opportunities with graduation standards, which are the standards all students must accomplish before graduating from high school in Minnesota. If educational change is to take place and students are to be successful, engaged learners, teachers must be knowledgeable about information and technology literacy skills. Media specialists must focus on the teachers because it is through them that we reach the students. The teacher is the door-keeper of these activities. (Mary Alice Anderson, personal communication, May 16, 1999)

There are excellent staff development programs being presented by library media specialists across the nation. Following are examples of these programs.

School-Level Library Media Staff Development Programs

Staff development in many school districts is provided at the district level as well as at the school level. One such school district is the Tucson Unified School District in Tucson, Arizona. Rebecca Jones, library media specialist at Gridley Middle School, is a teacher leader and resource liaison for her building to the district staff development program. She comments:

As resource liaison, I attend monthly meetings where district goals, standards, assessment, and other issues are discussed. Experts are brought in to provide us with specific strategies to increase achievement that we can take back to our building and share with teachers and staff. I meet monthly with our teachers and staff to provide them with materials and strategies that are immediately applicable to their classrooms. I am able to give them specific examples based on the units and topics they are using in their classrooms. The feedback has been positive, and many of these ideas are used and improved upon by our teachers. This liaison position has helped me develop curriculum partnerships with some teachers. (Rebecca Jones, personal communication, January 2, 1999)

Deborah Pendleton, media coordinator at Ligon Middle School, reports:

Although I have been involved in curricular-related staff development programs, most of our staff development has involved technology. Because the school became a part of a wide area network (WAN) over the past year, some technology-related needs were glaring to our school administration and to those of us (library media specialists and technology teachers) who were working with teachers on an individual basis. For example, assignments some teachers made involving the Internet showed a lack of understanding about what was available and how readily (or not) the information could be accessed. As a result, we did a staff development session on the effective use of Internet search engines at a recent teacher workday.

After presenting the in-service on Internet search engines, I was approached by numerous teachers to adapt my presentation for their students. This allowed me the opportunity to open doors to collaboration with teachers who had been reluctant to work closely with the media center in the past. For this presentation to be successful teachers and students had to be able to apply it to current or future topics of study. Not only did this open up communication between the teachers and me, it also opened up dialogue within teams of teachers. (Deborah Pendleton, personal communication, February 2, 1999)

A School-Level Staff Development Program

School 45 is an inner-city school in the Buffalo Public Schools in Buffalo, New York. It has an enrollment of 1,200 students, 600 of whom are limited English proficient representing 28 languages and 32 ethnic groups. The principal, in collaboration with a staff development faculty committee, surveyed the staff each spring to determine what programs should be offered during the following academic year.

The principal fostered staff development by providing program opportunities during school hours, at the school, with classroom coverage provided by substitute teachers and/or teacher aides. The principal attended all or part of each program, encouraged teachers to apply techniques learned, and arranged a follow-up session and/or further instruction.

Nancy E. Barnwell, library media specialist at School 45, describes her role as a staff developer:

The survey revealed that a program needed to be planned on decoding skills, and the principal asked me to design and deliver two sessions with eight K–2 staff members each. The objectives follow: Each participant will be able to identify at least four reading strategies they themselves use to find meaning in a literary selection; use at least three emergent reader strategies in their classroom during the first two weeks after the staff development program; and incorporate at least five of the emergent reader strategies into their continuing professional development.

I gave each participant a picture book in a language other than English. Their task was to read the book, using decoding strategies, and be able to "read" the book in English to another participant. I was available to help with decoding. Each participant explained his or her story to another.

It was a very successful lesson. Each participant was very proud of the new words they learned and how much of the story they could tell. They listed the reading strategies they employed to decode the story. The principal was an active participant. Each staff member made a commitment to introduce and/or apply at least three of the reading strategies when supervising children's reading of trade books. The principal suggested, and everyone concurred, that the group would meet in two weeks time for coffee and goodies before school in the library media center, to evaluate the application of the strategies in their classroom. This building staff development opportunity was also used successfully for a district-wide presentation and in a regional staff development program. (Nancy E. Barnwell, personal communication, December 7, 1998)

In two weeks' time, each of the teachers shared their accomplishment on the objectives and felt they had made very good progress. This is an excellent example of one program embedded in a cohesive, schoolwide staff development program.

A District-Level Library Media Staff Development Program

In June of each year the library media specialists of the Buffalo Public Schools in Buffalo, New York, completed an evaluation of the staff development program for that year. At the same time, they also completed a needs assessment for the coming year. Both documents were reviewed and collated in the office of the director of school library media services in preparation for a planning meeting of library media specialists held during the summer. Library media specialists selected ten to twelve representatives to serve on this committee. Through a consensus-building activity, the group did the preliminary planning for the eight staff development meetings that were held annually, in response to the evaluations of the previous year's program and the needs identified by the staff for the coming year. The end result was a cohesive and comprehensive staff development program for library media specialists.

Collegiality and cooperation developed among library media specialists, providing one another with expertise, support, resources, new ideas, and friendship. They found that the collective understanding about a problem and its possible solutions was better than the understanding of a single person. Library media specialists did not feel isolated but were part of a cohesive whole that had a vision, mission, goals, and objectives. This energy, direction, and accomplishment gave library media specialists pride and a knowledge that they were capable of making positive change in the instructional program for students. When presented with a challenge, they had many peers to call on for coaching and ideas. Most came to meetings with bags of resources for people who called beforehand and exchanged them for others they had requested. The meetings were an excellent networking opportunity.

A School Library System–Level
Library Media Staff Development Program

In 1986, Nassau School Library System, Nassau County, New York, embarked on a leadership development initiative for 56 school districts, including 328 public and private schools that were members of the system under the leadership of Carol Kroll, director of the system. The Nassau School Library System (NSLS) is one of 46 school library systems created by the New York State legislature in January 1985. These systems have the responsibility "to serve their member libraries by enabling them to improve services to their users, and to serve as components of the statewide library network, developing ways for all types of libraries to share resources through cooperation and coordination" (Kroll, 1994, 70).

The leadership development initiative was created as a result of responses from library media specialists to a needs assessment in which they shared a general feeling of dissatisfaction with the regard for library media specialists and a general lack of staff development activity at the school level. A planning team composed of thirty-five library media specialists, two superintendents, and the director of NSLS, Carol Kroll, determined that they would need to be proactive in changing the perception and role of library media specialists. After a review of the literature and much reflection and discussion, the team decided to create a different type of staff development that would be based on a peer support network. The objective of this unique program was to "ensure that media specialists could—and would—function as full-fledged faculty members and become part of the school's leadership team" (Kroll, 1994, 71).

They named their initiative Networks Enriching Teaching (NET) and contracted with Dr. Kenneth Tewel, a professor at Queens College, to train the library media specialists to be facilitators. They used these facilitation skills to cluster members in a region, plan meetings, create a welcoming atmosphere, encourage participation, support the goal of improving library media services, and establish a vehicle for mutual support. They continued to receive training in group process and educational pedagogy while they served as mentors for other library media specialists within the county. After eleven years, close to 100 library media specialists have received facilitator training and hundreds more have been involved in this peer support network. Led by the facilitators, groups meet every six weeks to discuss challenges, derive solutions, and share accomplishments. Through this process, library media specialists have changed their own perceptions about the role and mission of the library media center. As a result, they have been able to articulate and demonstrate a vision of the library media program for administrators and teachers in their schools, and they have made the vision a shared one whereby people in the school work toward its attainment. These accomplishments include state-of-the-art library media centers that are changing the way teachers teach as well as the way students learn and are assessed. Library media specialists are developing partnerships with classroom teachers and gaining respect and trust from administrators and the larger learning community. This has been evidenced by district superintendents providing increased support for the library media programs (Kroll, 1994, 71).

This model has been replicated in other regions in New York State as well as in the country. In 1991 the School Library Association of Western New York developed a similar program using the NSLS model for peer support, which continues to function successfully today. The NET concept has spawned other initiatives also, including a leadership training model for members of the School Library Media Section (SLMS) of the New York Library Association. From 1990 to 1994, thirty library media specialists were trained each year in leadership skills (one representative from each of the affiliates). These facilitators returned to their affiliate, where they developed peer support groups with the goal of implementing the guidelines presented in *Information Power* (AASL & AECT, 1988). The evaluation of this program confirmed that these people who had been trained in leadership skills were taking a leadership role in their schools, within their affiliate, and in the state organization and were attending national conferences where they were sharing their expertise through committee work.

Carol Kroll notes that the program in Nassau County continues to function and expand:

Yes, it is very much alive and well. This year we added a cluster group devoted to the implementation of *Information Power: Building Partnerships for Learning* [AASL & AECT, 1998] and to understanding how changes in program can take place. This year we are working with an AASL Task Force on the development of an Assessment Rubric for school library media programs. The Rubric will become our self-assessment Member Plan required by the State Education Department, New York State. Nassau School Library System members continue to identify NET as the single most significant service offered by NSLS. The process is as vital today as it was when we first developed it. (Carol Kroll, personal communication, April 19, 1999)

REDEFINING STAFF DEVELOPMENT

Staff development is being redefined as a result of three ideas that are transforming educational programs across the nation: results-driven education, systems thinking, and constructivism (Sparks, 1994, 26). As this newly defined staff development builds on and expands the positive characteristics of staff development just described, the focus will change from the teacher to the student. These changing trends can uniquely alter the manner in which library media specialists design and deliver staff development.

Results-driven education evaluates the effectiveness of a student's education, not by the courses taken or the grades earned but by what the student knows as a result of his or her years in school. The effectiveness of staff development will be evaluated not by the number of programs offered and participants attending but by the changes these teachers and administrators make to the instructional process that promote improvement in a student's academic achievement (26).

Systems thinking acknowledges that there is an interrelationship between and among parts of the system and that when these parts work together they create something bigger and more intricate than the individual parts. System thinkers can see how these parts interact and influence one another, resulting in support or obstruction. If change occurs in one area without consideration to its relationship to others, it could have a detrimental effect. Systems thinking promotes staff development increasingly driven by comprehensive strategic plans rather than by isolated programming (27).

Constructivism is a philosophy under which students "build knowledge structures rather than merely receive them from teachers" (27).

Knowledge is "constructed" in the mind of students. Instead of using the present practices of informing and directing, constructivist teachers model, guide, and provide a variety of learning activities and examples from which students build knowledge. Likewise, staff development programs based on constructivism feature teachers and administrators collaborating with each other as well as students in building knowledge and skills around solving instructional problems relevant to their setting rather than relying on a single session with an outside expert. The building of internal expertise and capacity to solve instructional problems has great potential for library media programs to flourish.

Results-driven education, systems thinking, and constructivism are changing the manner in which staff development is implemented.

- Programs are directed at the individual as well as the organization. In the past, programs were developed to help the individual do his or her job better. However, for students to be successful, programs must help both the individual and the organization to learn and solve problems, thereby enabling the organization to renew itself (27).

- Programs flow from a cohesive strategic plan for the district, school, and department rather than from a piecemeal approach that addresses a single concept. In the past, change was fragmented and often teachers had not yet achieved mastery of one concept before the district moved on to another. For students to be successful, there must be strategic planning at all levels, powerful vision and mission statements, and measurable goals and objectives toward which all areas of the learning community are working (27–28).

- Programs focus on the needs of the school rather than the needs of the district. Although districtwide needs are important, it is critical that staff development help the individual school achieve its goals and objectives. As this is accomplished, the district's goals and objectives will also be achieved. For students to be successful, the staff of the school must direct its attention to goals and objectives unique to that school (28).

- Programs provide job-embedded learning opportunities rather than training that teachers attend away from their classrooms under the direction of "experts." Teachers and administrators continually work to make the instructional program more effective. Teachers spend a greater amount of the work day involved in processes and activities that help them to constantly improve the instructional program (28). They are involved in study and learning as a result of conducting action research projects, participating in study or problem-solving groups, being a member of a peer coaching team, going on field trips, giving presentations at conferences, keeping a teacher reflection log/journal, taking university courses, participating in job exchanges, writing articles for journals, and collaborating in curriculum development and other improvement opportunities within the school and school district (Champion, 1998, 1).

- Programs focus on the needs of students and learning outcomes rather than on the needs of teachers and administrators. For students to be successful, teachers must focus on what students need to know and be able to do; only then can teachers identify the knowledge, skills, and attitudes teachers and administrators must acquire to enable students to be successful (Sparks, 1994, 28).

• Programs are designed so that superintendents, curriculum supervisors, principals, teacher leaders, and others see themselves as teachers of adults and accept this as an important part of their responsibility rather than delegating it to one or two departments. Once many people accept the responsibility for staff development, the staff development department becomes even more important. Members of the department provide training and ongoing support to administrators and teachers as they gain the knowledge and skills necessary to function in this new role, assist them through one-to-one coaching, and act as facilitators for meetings that are best handled by someone outside the school. These people function as consultants, planners, and facilitators, among other roles (28–29).

• Programs include all members of the learning community who have an impact on student learning, rather than just the teacher, which has been the focus in the past. For students to be successful, all these people must continually improve their knowledge base and skills so they can model them for students (29).

CONCLUSION

To be an effective participant in and provider of staff development, you as a library media professional must:

• Make a commitment to be a lifelong learner and model this behavior for students and members of the learning community. You will always have ideas around which to share and create visions as well as topics from which to build staff development programs.

• Demonstrate leadership skills and develop an effective, informal staff development program. Recognize that many services you presently provide to teachers are really staff development activities. Use them to move teachers to the next level of instructional service.

• Be proactive as a teacher leader and become a member of the staff development committee for your school and district, thereby impacting on the quality of staff development presented as well as influencing its content.

• Network ideas, resources, strategies, and more with peers, always strengthening the library media program and, therefore, improving student achievement.

• Begin to integrate the qualities of a redefined staff development program in your programming as well as the programming of your school and district. The focus is on the student.

• Be passionate in what you believe the library media program can contribute to the instructional program and how it impacts on students' ability to be information literate as well as successful in the 21st century.

- Become expert in all aspects of technology through staff development. Share this expertise through staff development, which you teach.

- Participate in LM_NET, an online exchange of questions and possible solutions from library media specialists around the country and world. You will be able to share challenges and receive suggestions for how others have handled the same problem. To subscribe, send an e-mail message to <LISTSERV @LISTSERV.SYR.EDU>. Then send the command SUBSCRIBE LM_NET followed by your first and last name, in that order.

- Use a variety of staff development activities, including distance learning (which allows you to take many courses, including work on an advanced degree, from the comfort of your computer in the home or office). All these opportunities will help you redefine staff development in your school.

Advocacy: Redefining a Community of Supporters

8

Recently at a meeting of a local library media association, two library media specialists were discussing their programs. They each worked in different school districts. Patricia, from the Mountain School District, was very excited about the inroads she has made in becoming a curriculum partner with teachers because of the resources she has been able to purchase, borrow through interlibrary loan, and retrieve from the Internet. Betty, from the Plains School District, was very disheartened because she felt she was making little progress with teachers and students primarily because her annual budget was very small. Furthermore, although there were computers in the school, there were none in the library media center. Patricia asked Betty if she had an advocacy program. Betty admitted that she did not but went on to say that she was just too busy to add one more task to her already unbelievably full day. Then she added, "What is involved in developing an advocacy program, and do you think it would make a difference in the program I can offer to my students and teachers?"

Patricia suggested that in everything she does, she feels she is influencing administrators, teachers, students, or parents. She said that she could either (1) influence them positively or negatively, or (2) in the words of Gary Hartzell, reinforce the notion of the "invisible librarian" (1994, 12). Patricia explained that because of the nature of their work and, especially, the fact that often the people with whom they work consider them to be support staff, they need to make themselves and their work more visible. She also said that she worked to positively influence people to build advocates for her program. Patricia asked Betty if she felt that her staff thought the library media program was an essential component of what the teachers are doing in their classrooms. Betty thought about it for a long time. When she answered, she indicated that generally she felt very comfortable with her staff and that occasionally when she asks teachers to plan with her for some program or help in some other way, they do so. However, she also had to admit that few people sought her out or asked for her assistance. She also told Patricia that she has asked several times for computers for the library media center but that the principal still has not approved them. Patricia asked what rationale she used when requesting the computers. Betty acknowledged that she had given no rationale because the principal already knows the library media center should have computers. Patricia asked Betty if she was computer literate, if she owned a computer, and if she used it in her work. As an example, she asked Betty if she used it for newsletters and memos that she sent to her staff. Betty did not have a computer, nor did she have a newsletter; when she needed to communicate with staff members she wrote them a note.

By now Betty had grown silent. Patricia suggested that all library media specialists must spend time each day discussing the importance of the library media program to the instructional program and its impact on student learning—in other words, advocating for their program. Betty had to concede that she had not been very proactive in this regard. She felt everyone already knew how important the library media center was to the instructional program. Patricia reinforced the thought that everything we do in our program impacts the advocacy people are willing to offer. She said, "We need to evaluate the way we interact with and respond to others, ensuring that our influence is active and not passive, positive and not negative." Patricia suggested that if Betty's principal had documentation for the types of resources and equipment that were needed and how they would be used to strengthen the instructional program, as funds became available he would be more inclined to allocate those funds to the library media center. She told Betty that if she advocated for her program, she could improve the program she was able to deliver to students and teachers.

This conversation continued for some time, with Betty beginning to develop an advocacy plan. Unfortunately, Betty's scenario is being played out in schools across the nation. These situations must be viewed as opportunities for each of us to become proactive as a leader and an agent of change to create a community of advocates for our library media program as well as library media programs around the world.

HOW CAN I DEVELOP AN ADVOCACY PLAN?

Advocacy begins with each library media specialist helping members of his or her learning community understand the mission of the library media program and its importance to the instructional program. Advocacy is built by influencing one person or group at a time. Being knowledgeable about the research that supports an effective library media program is important in developing an advocacy network of support.

The Library Media Specialist as Advocate

The library media specialist at the building level must be the first advocate for the library media program. We know our program, collection, students, teachers, and administrators. We also know how these variables blend to create a learning environment and instructional program within which students are active learners. We must positively influence the people with whom we work—the staff, administration, students, parents, and the community, thereby building advocacy for the library media program. We must build an influence bank at a time when we need nothing in exchange but will be able to draw on it in time of need. Library media specialists must be unified so that people will recognize the importance of the program to student learning and the ability to be successfully functioning adults in the 21st century. If we do not advocate for the library media program, others will feel it is not important.

Research

Once we accept the challenge to advocate for our program, we must become conversant with the research that supports an effective library media program. We must be able to discuss this research with administrators, teachers, parents, central office staff, and legislators—in person, through correspondence, at professional conferences, and in professional journals (for educators other than library media specialists). The research is threefold: Lance, Welborn, and Hamilton-Pennell (1992) define a strong library media program with adequate staff and collection; Krashen (1993) describes the benefits of a library media program to reading achievement; and Haycock (1992) gives an overview of research on almost any topic relative to school library media programming. This research is described more fully in the Introduction to this text.

An advocacy program must function on several levels: within the school and school community, within the larger learning community, within the political arena, and within the professional community. Each level is equally important; none can be overlooked. The following discussion reviews ideas at each level that can be incorporated in an advocacy plan. Additional resources are *Building Influence for the School Librarian* (Hartzell, 1994) and *Program Advocacy: Power, Publicity, and the Teacher-Librarian* (Haycock, 1990).

WITHIN THE SCHOOL AND SCHOOL COMMUNITY

In essence, an advocacy program encompasses everything we do. Each time we speak to a student, teacher, parent, or administrator, we are impacting advocacy. Remember that we can influence each individual positively or negatively, or we can reinforce the concept of "the invisible librarian."

The Library Media Specialist

The library media specialist must create opportunities to advocate for the media center program, continually adding to the advocacy network.

David Sanger, library media specialist at Baker Middle School in Denver, Colorado, shares several strategies that he has utilized to his advantage when advocating for his library media program:

Initially, I used David Loertscher's collection mapping to demonstrate how Library Power funding impacted the library media collection. This information was shared with the National Library Power organization as well as with our school-level Library Power Leadership Committee composed of the principal, a teacher, student, parent, and myself. This was excellent information for the Leadership Committee, providing direction for collection development.

While this was the first time I used this process, collection mapping continues to assist me in developing the library media collection. When a teacher comes to plan a unit, I immediately build a map of what is available in our media center.

I also have used mapping when advocating for the annual library media budget. For the past three years, I created several collection maps and presented them to our Collaborative Decision Making Team, which makes the decisions on budget and is composed of the principal, teachers, parents, and a business representative. I compared the size of our collection and expenditure per pupil for library media resources with the state average. I was able to demonstrate that our students did not have equitable access to information. The average school in Colorado had seventeen books per pupil. We had only twelve. The decision-making team has provided an annual budget increase to work toward equity. At the time I prepared the first collection map, the library media allocation was $3,500. Within two years, the annual allocation more than doubled. These maps have made a significant difference in the library media program.

I discovered that collection maps can help me advocate for teacher use of library media resources as well. Many teachers participate in the collection development process by suggesting specific titles or areas of the collection that need strengthening. When a new order is received, teachers are interested in learning what has arrived. Recently I received a $5,000 order. I was able to show where the dollars were spent: 28 percent on colonial American history, 14 percent on technology, 10 percent on biography, and so forth. Several teachers immediately came to the media center to collaborate on a project to use the new materials.

Additionally, I have been a successful advocate for our library media program outside our school district. Using a map showing the weakest area of our collection, I received $14,000 from a Library Service and Technology Act (LSTA) grant to build our print and technology resource collection in the area of mathematics. In addition, the Public Education and Business Alliance, in Colorado, provides grants of $1,000 for literacy-related projects and $2,000 for technology-related projects. We won five of these grants this year as a result of teachers and myself collaborating on collection development and instruction, thus strengthening our instructional program.

Finally, there was a serious school budget problem a few years ago. Each school received a list of possible areas where program could be cut. The library media program was on that list. When we attended a meeting to discuss this problem, the parent member of the Collaborative Decision Making Team (CDMT) stood up and said, "I don't know where we are going to cut, but I do know where we are not going to cut and that is the library media program." She had been a part of creating the program and collection, saw the value to students, and was willing to advocate for the library media program. Our budget and program remained intact. (David Sanger, personal communication, June 11, 1999)

The strategies that David is using are easily replicated. David Loertscher's *Collection Mapping in the LMC: Building Access in a World of Technology* (1996) is a valuable tool. These maps can provide the documentation for why a given collection needs additional funds. Of course, the maps are built only after thoroughly "weeding" the collection so that it is current and meets the needs of students. David's story about the parent who advocated for the library media program is the ultimate advocacy. David had a vision; this parent understood and believed in the vision and made it her own; then she worked so that nothing would detract from the vision.

Students

Students will be a powerful block of advocates in the future if they feel the present program is worthy of their advocacy. Although this forceful group may not be available for a few years, once they begin to vote on budgets or bond issues they will have an impact on staffing levels and resources. If they have had an exemplary program and feel they are valued individuals, they will step forward and advocate for students by supporting the library media program.

There are many ways beyond the day-to-day interaction with students that we can influence them and help them remember the library media program. For example, just as we participate in activities outside the library media center to influence teachers and administrators, we should view this type of activity as an opportunity to influence students as well. Volunteer to be a class or club advisor. Become part of the team that goes to a feeder school to welcome prospective students or provide orientation to students when they arrive at the new school. Develop a tutorial program that takes place in the library media center—students who have a strength in particular subjects become tutors for students needing assistance. This can take place before or after school as well as during the school day. Such a program will increase the visibility of the library media center, raise the tutors' image of themselves, and help them begin a service of volunteerism that might continue throughout their lifetime.

These are just a few ideas to get you started. Students will remember these experiences with the library media specialist and the library media program. Consider the following story about a librarian and how she interacted with a child in her school. In 1965, Blanche H. Caffiere was a school librarian at the View Ridge Elementary School in Seattle, Washington.

I was approached one day by a fourth grade teacher. She described a boy who needed a challenge; he finished his work so quickly. "Could he slip into the library and help?" she asked. There's always work to do in the library, so I said, "Send the little guy in."

Soon a slight fellow in blue jeans and a blue T-shirt appeared. "Do you have a job for me? My name is Bill." . . . I proceeded to tell him a little about the Dewey Decimal system and the arrangement of nonfiction books by numbers on the shelves. He picked up the idea immediately and said, "And the fiction ones are arranged alphabetically by the author's last name."

He may have looked like other nine-year-olds, but his zeal set him apart. . . . I had hardly launched into the problems of misplaced "copy-2" cards in "copy-1" book pockets when he said, "is it kind of a detective job?" I agreed, and he became an unrelenting sleuth.

He had found three books with wrong cards when his teacher opened the door and announced, "Time for recess, Bill." He argued for finishing the job at hand; she made the case for fresh air. She won, and he reluctantly joined his classmates.

The next morning, he arrived early. "I wanted to finish yesterday's job—finding those missing books," he said. When he asked to be a regular librarian, it was easy to say yes. He worked untiringly, never stopping to talk to other children. After a few weeks, I found a beflowered note on my desk. Bill stood by grinning as I opened an invitation to dinner at his home.

At the end of a delightful evening, Bill's mother made a surprising announcement. The family would be moving to the adjoining school district. She said Bill's first concern was, "I can't leave View Ridge library. Who will find the lost books?" But when the time came, his teacher, his classmates, and I said our reluctant goodbyes to Bill. Though he had initially seemed a somewhat ordinary kid, I now regarded him as a sharp little character.

I missed his early-morning arrivals, but not for long. A few days later, in the door he popped. He stood at the entrance and joyfully announced, "The librarian over there doesn't let boys work in the library. My mother got me transferred back to View Ridge for the rest of the year. My dad will drop me off on his way to work. And if he can't, I'll walk!"

I suppose I should have had some inkling that this kind of focused determination would take him wherever he wanted to go. What I could not have guessed was that he would become the electronics wizard of the age: Bill Gates, tycoon of Microsoft. (Caffiere, 1995, 17, reprinted with permission from the author)

This wonderful story is a dramatic reminder that advocates are built with each encounter we have with every member of the learning community.

Parents

If students are excited about an activity in the library media center they will discuss it at home with their parents, who will, over time, become supportive of the library media specialist as well as the program. For approximately fifteen years in one large city school district, every time there was a budget crisis the list of nonmandated programs was put on the table and, generally, cut. The library media program seemed to be on the top of that list. Each year a very large group of parents would attend weekly Board of Education meetings to request that the library media program not be cut, giving specific reasons for maintaining it at the present level or increasing it. Students spoke regularly also, describing how they made use of the library media program. Some evenings as many as two hundred people called the Board office and asked to speak. The first fifty speakers would be scheduled. However, the presence of the overflow crowd spoke volumes about the support of the program and advocacy. Except for one time, the positions were always replaced. Parents advocated for the library media program because the dedicated staff of library media specialists were passionate about the importance of the program and its benefits to the children's instructional program. There were always many people who were willing to write letters, call the City Council and Board of Education members, speak before a Board of Education or Common Council meeting, or contact state and national legislators. Parents as advocates constitute a powerful voice.

A Library Volunteer Program is another avenue for developing advocates. People who volunteer in the library media center may be considering a return to the work force. This volunteer experience will help them make that decision. Some volunteers, such as retired educators, grandparents, and others, are in it for the long term; others are testing the waters for future employment. We can be grateful for the assistance of every volunteer, appreciate and make use of their talents while they are with us, and then wish them well as they go on to another part of their lives. We hope we have created an advocate who knows how the program contributes to the instruction of students and will be an active supporter.

Reading motivational programs, special celebrations, multicultural fairs, and other activities promote a relationship between the library media program and the home that will develop advocacy through positive influence on both the student and the parents.

A Special Story of Advocacy

We have discussed the need to establish a partnership with the administrator and teachers. We have also talked about the need to create an influence bank with all members of the learning community, including students and parents. Remember, the way in which you interact with each individual will determine the way he or she feels about you and may affect the intensity of advocacy provided. We never know where a student, administrator, teacher, or parent will be or what position he or she may hold in the future relative to the well-being of our program as well as our profession.

The anecdote that follows demonstrates the influence a project can have on students, teachers, administrators, and parents—all of whom are potential advocates for the library media program in the future.

Trudy Gurn is the library media specialist at McKinley High School, one of the Buffalo Public Schools in Buffalo, New York. McKinley has a student enrollment of 1,200 and draws its students from all sections of the city. Trudy Gurn, together with Luciana Harrigan, bilingual teacher, and Mark J. Walter, computer resource teacher, advocated for a group of students when they applied for an ESL (English as Second Language) state grant. Trudy describes the program:

One day while Luciana, Mark, and myself were collaborating on a project for students in Luciana's classes, she mentioned that she had just received information on a granting opportunity. We identified needs of this group of students and then brainstormed ideas that would address these needs.

Bilingual students attending our school had little knowledge about the larger community of Buffalo or the cultural agencies within this community that would provide them with lifelong learning skills. Although they came to school each day, they generally took a bus from their community to school and home again with few occasions to explore the area outside their immediate community. Although the bilingual students had friends in school, there was little opportunity for them to continue their friendship beyond the school day unless these friends were from their neighborhood. In addition, they had little opportunity to use technology, including the latest equipment in photography and printing, during the classes in which they were enrolled and required to take. With these needs in mind, we wrote a grant that both addressed the needs and included specific

New York State Standards in the areas of writing, reading, critical thinking, and technology.

This successful Bilingual Excel grant, in which students made application to participate, provided opportunities for forty students to learn basic skills such as how to read a street map as well as critical thinking and problem-solving skills. Students planned a tour of their community using a variety of modes of transportation. Through field trips in which students visited the public libraries, the art and historical museums, horticultural gardens, and a butterfly conservatory, they learned to describe and differentiate among the functions of each of these agencies and sites while improving their effective social communication in English. They gained an understanding of the social, historical, and cultural diversities within their communities by using various print and technology resources. Students applied learned technological knowledge and skills to design a Web page with the assistance of a consultant. As a result of working cooperatively with other students throughout this project, they developed cross-cultural skills and an understanding as well as an appreciation of one another.

In this after-school program, each student maintained a journal, writing in it often on field trips and during instruction. For example, at the historical museum, students were asked to focus on the changes that the city of Buffalo experienced and then write about the transformations they witnessed in the exhibits that included their countrymen. Writing in their journals helped them complete this assignment. As a result of an art appreciation class, students selected a painting from available art books and wrote a critique in their journals, which were later presented to classmates. While at the art gallery, students described their impressions and wrote commentaries in their journals about one of Monet's paintings. They recorded their observations and took photographs of the sites with single use cameras. These journal articles and photographs became the source of information as they wrote articles that were word processed and eventually uploaded onto their Internet Web page. Join us on our Web page at <http://www.buffnet.net/~macklib>.

Technology was an important New York State Standard addressed through this grant. Students used a variety of technology sources including online databases to do research and word processing to write articles, summarize field trips, and write captions for their photographs.

In the last phase of the program, using their journal entries and notes, students wrote about what they learned from this Bilingual Excel grant experience. A few of their anecdotes follow: "I saw things and went places I have never been to or seen before." "I met new people in our group, which made me feel good and work harder." "I learned about Buffalo's history and I am telling you, if you get time to study Buffalo, you will find how historically important it is." "This is a great program that I have joined. It helps students to improve their writing skills, learn more English, and meet other bilingual students. The teachers were working very hard to help students achieve their very best."

Students were assessed on their journal entries; the types of articles they chose; their note taking and capability to synthesize information; their performance in using technology and their skill to locate specific information on the Internet; their ability to work in cooperative groups; and the final edition of the Internet Web page.

The evaluation of the project was based on teacher observation, student reflections, photograph quality, and inclusion of articles on the Web page. Most of the teachers involved in the project as well as classroom teachers observed many changes in the quality of student work and their participation in class. However, the most noticeable change was in the affective domain. Students developed a sense of self-importance that was not evident at the beginning of the project. Many students formed new friendships, which although still developed primarily along cultural lines, oftentimes included students of diverse cultures. (Trudy Gurn, Luciana Harrigan, & Mark J. Walter, personal communication, June 15, 1999)

This example of an after-school activity in which students learned while having fun describes an experience in which the library media specialist in collaboration with colleagues (and having the support of the administrator as well as the involvement of teachers and parents) advocated for students, who in turn will advocate for school library media centers and schools in the future. Developing positive experiences in schools will make positive adults who support the library media center and education.

Library Media Advisory Committee

Another way of bringing members of the learning community together for the advancement of the library media program is to establish a Library Media Advisory Committee. As you broaden the base of support for and "ownership" of the library media program, a Library Media Advisory Committee composed of teachers, students, parents, and administrators will help to develop and maintain an exemplary program while adding to your network of advocates. Members of this committee can assist in many tasks that communicate the importance of the library media program within the instructional program.

Board of Education Members

Members of the Board of Education are very influential people who control the funding as well as program decisions within your school district. They should be included in your advocacy plan. Invite them to be a guest speaker, an honored guest, or a judge when the library media center is celebrating School Library Media Month or other special occasions. Find ways to be supportive of their positions and interests. Help them understand the importance of the library media program to the academic achievement of students. Share research and practical experiences about the program. Develop a relationship with these people when there is no real need. Then, when there is a need, they may work harder to resolve the problem because they feel they have already become advocates of the library media program. Also recognize that they are contacted by many individuals in the community and the school district with specific requests. It may take several overtures to begin to develop a relationship.

District-Level Advocacy

One of the strengths of the library media program at the district level derives from a unified, cohesive program that demonstrates systematic growth and is directed by a library media leader at the district level. If your district does not have a leadership position for the library media/technology department, an advocacy program should be undertaken to establish such a position. This advocacy is the responsibility of every member of the department as well as members of your advocacy network.

Additionally, just as it is critical to have creative, passionate, and competent library media specialists in each media center, it is equally imperative that there be creative, passionate, competent, and supportive former library media specialists in administrative positions. Carolyn Giambra is a library media specialist who has accepted an administrative position, that of district instructional specialist, for the Williamsville Central School District in Williamsville, New York. Carolyn has several responsibilities for the instructional program, the library media program being one of them. She has been an advocate for the library media program as a library media specialist and continues that role in her position in the central office.

Carolyn Giambra gives two examples of how she has been able to advocate successfully for school library media programs in the Williamsville Schools by listening, reflecting, and responding to the needs of others:

During this past year, there were several issues involving members within our learning community when, because I listened carefully to others and reflected on their concerns, I was able to wrap some of the library media needs into someone else's agenda. One of our assistant superintendents was discussing the need to purchase parenting resources again. He indicated that they were always losing these materials. I was able to point out that each of the library media centers already had a small parenting collection and if the resources he was discussing were part of this collection, they would be circulated in the same manner as the rest of the collection, which should cut down on the loss of resources. The assistant superintendent asked psychologists and social workers to create a list of parenting resources, which library media specialists purchased. Besides the new resources, which were important additions, funding came from a source other than the library media budget, and the materials brought new people in to use the media center. This provided additional resources while helping to solve the assistant superintendent's problem.

Another situation in which I was able to advocate for library media programs was in the resolution to a problem with current technology. We ran our periodical indexes and other CD-ROM products on a tower that had not been updated for several months. The work load of our technicians was so heavy they were unable to schedule the task. It was October, and the last update was the previous May. Over the summer, several high profile events took place to which students needed access. After sharing these concerns with the supervisor in charge, I learned that the technicians felt that the technology was outdated and that it would be easier to manage if the databases were online. Although this was not the solution I initially sought, the one finally agreed on was much more advantageous to teachers, students, and library media specialists. This was a situation where patience, discussion of the issues, and an investment of time provided a solution for the technicians as well as their supervisor and an excellent resolution to our problem.

When I advocate for the library media program, I am looking for ways of helping other people satisfy their agenda items. An advocate needs to be patient, a careful listener, read everything that crosses his or her desk, observe what is going on in the organization, know his or her facts and be prepared at all times, never exaggerate or misrepresent an issue, and spend time reflecting on how the library media program can become part of the solutions of others. (Carolyn Giambra, personal communication, May 18, 1999)

WITHIN THE LARGER LEARNING COMMUNITY

The larger learning community is another important target from which to build advocacy. This will take many forms. Develop a partnership with your local public library, art gallery, or science and historical museums. Develop that partnership as both the library media specialist in your school and the friend of these cultural institutions. Join a "Friends of the Library" or "Literacy Volunteers" group, and volunteer as needed. Get appointed to boards of directors. Become known in your community as a force to improve the quality of life.

You may also choose to join a public service organization such as Rotary, Lions, or the Chamber of Commerce and share a special talent as well as your good humor. Getting to know people informally as you interact in completing a service to a group of people, if done competently and humbly, will influence the people with whom you are working. Alternatively, you might offer to present a program on your district's library media program at one of their meetings.

Become involved in mentoring programs, which are becoming more numerous across the country. Provide the space as well as other needs for these mentors as they work with students. You might volunteer at a community center and bring a special expertise. Select something in which you have an interest and feel comfortable. There are innumerable opportunities.

In this role of volunteer not only will you help others, but at some point they may help you by being a member of your advocacy network. Helping others at a time when you need nothing in exchange is like putting influence in the bank from which you can draw as necessary.

Becky Pasco is a library media specialist at Lincoln High School in Lincoln, Nebraska. Although she is a high school media specialist, she has made inroads into the community by volunteering in ethnic community centers to do story times in their day care centers once a month.

I leave goodies of some sort, bookmarks, stickers, and so forth, with our school logo for the little ones. I show up at their after-school homework programs every once in a while and offer mentoring or information services. I attend parent meetings at these ethnic centers and invite them to have their meetings in our library media center. When I know they are coming, I try to have a display of items from our collection that supports an agenda item or two about which they are concerned. Our school is very diverse, and my presence at these ethnic community centers is crucial in helping to establish a relationship between the cultural groups in our community and the high school where they send their most precious commodity every day—their children. (Becky Pasco, personal communication, January 2, 1999)

Becky is adding to her advocacy network as well.

Deann Sheppard is the library media specialist at Lorraine Academy, a grades 3–8 Buffalo Public School with an enrollment of 485 students in Buffalo, New York. School partnerships were created in the Buffalo School District several years ago with businesses and service organizations within the city. The Rotary Club of Buffalo established a mentoring program as one element of their partnership with Lorraine Academy. The mentoring program is located in the library media center. Deann describes this program and its outcomes:

There are forty mentors who are members of Rotary and come weekly to Lorraine Academy to work in the library media center with forty at-risk students who need additional assistance in reading, writing, mathematics, and social studies. They help students with research projects including searching the Internet for information. A major goal of the instructional program at Lorraine Academy is to improve both the reading and writing achievement of students. The objective of the mentors is to assist in the accomplishment of this goal by developing goals and objectives with their mentees and then helping them work to achieve them. The mentors encourage their mentees to read and write effectively. As part of this goal, the mentors model reading by reading with them each week from a book in the library media collection. They also maintain a journal as do the mentees, and use the journals to regularly communicate with each other.

The mentors have added a new dimension to the library media program. It is like having a large group of volunteers helping students learn. They have been an active part of our "Author Days" as well as our reading motivational programs such as "Read Across America." They have helped their mentees write their books and have encouraged them in the reading motivational programs as well. Mentors have also taken part in the culminating ceremonies for each of these programs.

Each of these mentors is involved in all aspects of our program, and they have become powerful advocates for our school. For example, mentors have spoken at Board of Education meetings in support of library media positions when these were in jeopardy; written "letters to the editor" when there was a concern within the school; and have become members of community committees to improve education. Because these mentors are working in our school, they are knowledgeable about the program as well as its needs. They have become advocates of the instructional as well as the library media programs, working to improve education in the Buffalo Public Schools. This mentoring program has been very successful for both the students and the adults. (Deann Sheppard, personal communication, August 4, 1999)

WITHIN THE POLITICAL ARENA

Traditionally, a relatively small percentage of library media specialists have tried to influence local, state, or national legislators to an understanding of the essential role of the library media specialist and program within the instructional program. Library media specialists may not have contacted legislators in the past because they felt intimidated and uncomfortable in this role. Perhaps they felt someone else was doing that job. Just as you must decide on your comfort level of participation in the politics of your school, you must decide this in the larger political sphere as well. However, as in school politics, so in the political arena—if you choose not to participate, you lose your ability to influence the situation; as a result, your students lose many advantages that legislation and other sources could provide.

Even though most state professional organizations as well as the American Library Association have an annual legislative day, it is most important to meet with legislators when they are at home in the local district, where they are more relaxed and attentive. Learn about their interests and support them, know their schedule and make an appointment to talk with them, give testimony at public hearings, and become known as a person who advocates for students and a quality instructional program of which the library media program is a foundation. Because state and national legislators spend a large share of their time in state or national offices, develop a relationship with the education staff person in the local office. The staff has the ear of the legislator and can be a very important advocate. Legislators spend much of their time out-side the district making decisions that affect the district. They need in-formation from which to make intelligent choices. Be one of the people who influence these legislators.

As a leader, you have a vision of your library media program. To attain this vision, additional funds may be necessary. You are dependent on Board of Education members, city and town council members, and state and national legislators for the fulfillment of your vision. Develop a relationship with these important people. To foster this relationship, think of ways of educating them about the role of the library media specialist and program. Using a state or national library media theme, extend an invitation to them to participate as an honored guest, speaker, or judge in a special reading program or other event in your media center. Participation in coffee hours and other programs sponsored by a local professional organization or school district can provide opportu-nities to influence them as well.

Regardless of the method, accept the challenge to include legislators in your advocacy plan. Speak to them about the library media specialists' role within education. That message must be articulated clearly, consis-tently, and often, and by as many library media specialists and other members of the learning community as possible.

Sandy Schuckett, library media teacher at El Sereno Middle School Library in Los Angeles, California; vice president for legislation, Califor-nia School Library Association; and chair of the Legislation Committee, AASL, offers sound advice.

Although there is a hesitancy on the part of some library media specialists to become politically involved, it is critical that each of us get out of our library and make an appointment to meet our legislators. We can learn about their in-terests, share a new book they might like, and ask if they would like to borrow it (don't worry if you do not get it back!). As you develop a relationship by showing interest in what is important to them, you can also share information about what is important to you—you can advocate for your library program. If you develop a good relationship with a legislator and look upon him or her as a friend, he or she will look upon you same way. And he or she will also perceive you as *the expert* on school library issues.

Once you have developed a relationship, it's a good idea to make contact with the legislator at least twice each year, and more often when there is an issue that requires his or her support. When there is a library-related issue for which the legislator must cast a vote, you are the one he or she will call on for advice. This occurs because by now he or she knows you, considers you to be a friend, and respects your position and professional expertise. And he or she will be more inclined to vote in support of the particular issue. This is exactly what happened a few years ago when one of my colleagues in California was contacted by the office of her U.S. Representative seeking advice on pending library legislation.

When my colleague asked her to vote in the affirmative, the Representative did so because of the relationship established prior to that vote.

Advocacy at the grassroots level is growing and needs your active involvement. It also needs the involvement of your teachers, students, and parents. When there is an issue that needs support, in addition to your phone calls and letters, encourage these members of the learning community to call, write letters, and send materials that will both describe and demonstrate how the library media specialist and program have benefited the academic achievement of students. (Sandy Schuckett, personal communication, October 18, 1999)

WITHIN THE PROFESSIONAL COMMUNITY

State and national library media organizations must become more proactive in targeting professional organizations other than library media such as school boards, parent teachers, reading teachers, and other disciplines to present programs highlighting the strengths of the library media program as well as the ways in which the program impacts the instructional program of students. Professional journals must be targeted as well. Exemplary library media programs must be shared by the media specialists conducting these programs, describing how they support particular subject or program areas as well as students.

The School Library Media Section (SLMS) of the New York Library Association has developed a multifaceted program to build influence for its members and to garner advocates. There are five segments to the program (Giambra, 1998, 18–19).

- First, there is a scripted presentation on the library media program that SLMS members can use in their local schools and communities with boards of education and parent groups.

- Second, there is a College Outreach Program based on the activities of the Kansas Association of School Librarians. In this program SLMS members contact college and university departments of education to offer a team of library media specialists to present the benefits of cooperative program planning and teaching between teachers and the library media specialist to preservice teachers. They are working to provide uniform coverage to all colleges and universities.

- The third segment targets professional conferences, mainly of decisionmakers. SLMS exhibits at these professional conferences, providing valuable information about library media programs.

- The fourth segment provides support for library media specialists within their learning community. If a school district has budget problems that threaten the position of library media specialist, SLMS conducts a "Letter to the Editor" campaign. The president of SLMS writes a letter to each newspaper in the village, town, or city (1) describing the benefits to student achievement of an effective library media program staffed by a certified library media specialist, and (2) requesting that the Board of Education not sacrifice this important program.

- The fifth segment of the program includes a "Letter to the Editor" to newsletters of state organizations. For example, a letter from a SLMS president was sent to the state American Federation of Teachers affiliate, New York State United Teachers (NYSUT,) thanking NYSUT for its support of mandating elementary library media specialists. Although the mandate was not approved, this letter generated several newsworthy opportunities for NYSUT to experience library media issues, resulting in a centerfold article on library media programs in its newsletter. Giambra states: "There are many advocates among us, with the passion to convey the message far and wide. Some lack the tools, some lack the confidence, and some lack a partner" (1998, 18–19). Each of us must advocate for library media programs as well as partner with someone else to advocate for similar programs in the larger learning community and within the political arena at the local, state, and national levels.

CONCLUSION

While Patricia, in the opening scenario, probably has an exemplary program for which she is an advocate, both Betty and Patricia must develop a specific advocacy plan. Although the majority of this chapter addresses developing advocacy within the school, each of us must move beyond the walls of our schools to the broader learning community, the political arena, and the professional community. It is not enough that someone else may be doing this. We must be visiting, communicating in writing, sending e-mail, and speaking on the telephone. We must present programs at professional conferences and publish articles in professional journals for people outside our profession as well as for the decision-makers in our community, state, and nation. We must influence one person at a time at all levels, thereby building a network of advocates. If we do this effectively, when there is a problem we will have credits in our influence bank from which to draw. Our professional lives as well as the life of our profession are depending on us.

Epilogue

At the heart of school reform is the improvement of teaching and learning. The library media program as presented in *Curriculum Partner: Redefining the Role of the Library Media Specialist* is central to that reform and can be the vehicle to accomplish this in every school in the nation.

Based on the evaluation report of the National Library Power Program (Dewitt Wallace, 1999), flexible scheduling and collaboration have had a positive impact on the teaching and learning process. These two components of program have changed the way teachers teach and students learn in many Library Power schools. The results show that the effort to become a curriculum partner is worth it. You have the tools—the steps, strategies, and techniques—needed to replicate these findings in your school.

Conduct a survey to determine what services and activities classroom teachers and students would like as part of the library media program. Start small. Select one or two improvements that will broaden the base of support and add to your advocacy network. Ultimately you will enjoy a full partnership with both the principal and the classroom teachers in which you are a team member in the planning, implementation, and assessment of the instructional program. In this atmosphere, school reform will flourish, and students will become information literate, lifelong learners, and successfully contributing adults in the 21st century. Although it will likely take many successful interactions with others to achieve this vision, a flexible program that is collaboratively planned with the classroom teacher is essential. The success of the students depends on you.

References

Achilles, C. M. (1987). A vision of better schools. In William Greenfield (Ed.), *Instructional leadership: Concepts, issues, and controversies* (pp. 17–37). Boston: Allyn and Bacon.

Ackerman, Richard H. (Ed.-in-chief). (1996). *Every teacher as a leader: Realizing the potential of teacher leadership.* Gayle Moller and Marilyn Katzenmeyer (Eds.). San Francisco: Jossey-Bass.

American Association of School Librarians. (n.d.). *Position statement on: Role of the library media specialist in site-based management.* Chicago: American Association of School Librarians.

American Association of School Librarians. (1999). *A Planning guide for information power: Building partnerships for learning with school library media program assessment rubric for the 21st century.* Chicago: American Association of School Librarians.

American Association of School Librarians and the Association for Educational Communications and Technology. (1988). *Information power: Guidelines for school library media programs.* Chicago: American Library Association.

American Association of School Librarians and the Association for Educational Communications and Technology. (1998). *Information power: Building partnerships for learning.* Chicago: American Library Association.

Angle, Melanie, et al. (1997). Nutrition. In *Teaching electronic information skills: A resource guide for grades 9–12* (pp. 1–13). McHenry, IL: Follett Software.

Archer, Jeff. (1998, October). The Link to higher scores. *Education Week, 18* (5), 10–11.

Armstrong, Thomas. (1994). *Multiple intelligences in the classroom.* Alexandria, VA: Association for Supervision and Curriculum Development.

Bellman, Geoffrey M. (1992). *Getting things done when you are not in charge: How to succeed from a support position.* San Francisco: Berrett-Koehler.

Bennis, Warren. (1989). *On becoming a leader.* Reading, MA: Addison-Wesley.

Berger, Pam. (1998). *Internet for active learners: Curriculum-based strategies for K–12*. Chicago: American Library Association.

Bernstein, Allison. (1997, May–June). Flexible schedules: Quality learning time. *Library Talk, 10* (3), p. 11.

Blake, Virgil L. P. (1996). The Virtual library impacts the school library media center: A bibliographic essay. In Carol Collier Kuhlthau (Ed.), *The Virtual school library: Gateway to the information superhighway* (pp. 3–19). Englewood, CO: Libraries Unlimited.

Blanchard, Ken, Carlos, John P., & Randolph, Alan. (1996). *Empowerment takes more than a minute*. San Francisco: Berrett-Koehler.

Bleakley, Anne, & Carrigan, Jackie L. (1994). *Resource-based learning activities: Information literacy for high school students*. Chicago: American Library Association

Bloom, Benjamin, S. (Ed.). (1956). Taxonomy of educational objectives: Classification of educational goals. New York: David McKay Company, Inc.

Boyer, Ernest L. (1995). *The basic school: A community for learning*. Princeton, NJ: Carnegie Foundation for the Advancement of Teaching.

Brevik, Patricia Senn, & Senn, J. A. (1993, September–October). Information literacy: Partnerships for power. *Emergency Librarian, 21* (1), pp. 25–28.

Brookfield, Stephen D. (1986). *Understanding and facilitating adult learning*. San Francisco: Jossey-Bass.

Brooks, Jacqueline Grennon, & Brooks, Martin G. (1993). *In search of understanding: The case for constructivist classrooms*. Alexandria, VA: Association for Supervision and Curriculum Development.

Brown, Robert, Deal, Barry, & Mycio, Geri. (1998). *Understanding change and transition*. Buffalo, NY: Continuous Improvement Strategies.

Brualdi, Ann. (1998, November–December). Gardner's theory. *Teacher Librarian, 26* (2), pp. 26–28.

Buchanan, Jan. (1991). *Flexible access library media programs*. Englewood, CO: Libraries Unlimited.

Caffiere, Blanche H. (1995, July 20). Hints of future heights in an extraordinary little boy. *The Christian Science Monitor*, p. 17.

California School Library Association. (1997). *From library skills to information literacy: A handbook for the 21st century* (2nd ed.). San Jose, CA: Hi Willow Research and Publishing.

Callison, Daniel. (1994). The potential for portfolio assessment. In Carol Collier Kuhlthau (Ed.), *Assessment and the school library media center* (pp. 121–130). Englewood, CO: Libraries Unlimited.

Callison, Daniel. (1998, January). Authentic assessment. *School Library Media Activities Monthly, 14* (5), pp. 42, 43, 50.

Champion, Robin. (1998, December). *35 options for professional development*. Washington, DC: National Staff Development Conference.

Chicago Board of Education. (1999). Elements of a scoring rubric. [On-line]. Available: <http://intranet.cps.k12.il.us/Assessments/Ideas_and_Rubrics/Intro_Scoring/intro_scoring.html>.

Clinton, William Jefferson. (1995, October 10). Remarks by the president in announcement of technology learning grants. Washington, DC: White House Office of the Press Secretary.

Coleman, Gordon J., Jr. (1993). Managing change. In Ben B. Carson & Jane Bandy Smith (Eds.), *Renewal at the schoolhouse: Management ideas for library media specialists and administrators* (pp. 75–84). Englewood, CO: Libraries Unlimited.

Covey, Stephen R. (1992). *Principle-centered leadership.* New York: Simon & Schuster.

Craver, Kathleen W. (1994). Emerging technologies: Applications and implications for school library media centers. Washington, DC: U.S. Department of Education.

Cross, Christopher T., & Joftus, Scott. (1997, Fall). U.S. educational system seeks wholesale reform. *Forum for Applied Research and Public Policy, 12* (3), pp. 72–77.

Curzon, Susan C. (1989). *Managing change: A how-to-do-it manual for planning, implementing, and evaluating change in libraries.* New York: Neal-Schuman Publishers.

Darish, John C. (1987). Administrator in-service: A route to continuous learning and growing. In William Greenfield (Ed.), *Instructional leadership concepts, issues, and controversies* (pp. 328–340). Boston: Allyn and Bacon.

DeGroff, Linda. (1997, Winter). *Perceptions of roles and relationships in the school library: A national survey of teachers, administrators, and library media specialists.* (Reading Research Report No. 72). Athens, GA: National Reading Research Center.

Dewitt Wallace Reader's Digest Fund. (1999). *Executive summary: Findings from the evaluation of the National Library Power Program.* Madison: University of Wisconsin at Madison School of Library and Information Studies and School of Education.

Dilenschneider, Robert I.. (1990). *Power and influence: Mastering the art of persuasion.* New York: Prentice-Hall.

Dobrez, Cynthia K., & Rutan, Lynn M. (1996, May–June). Making friends in high places. *The Book Report, 16,* pp. 13, 15.

Doiron, Ray. (1993, September–October). Teachers and teacher-librarians exploring curriculum potential. *Emergency Librarian, 21* (1), pp. 9–16.

Donham, Jean. (1998). Assessment of information processes and products. In *Follett's Professional Development Series.* McHenry, IL: Follett Software.

Dorrell, Larry D., & Lawson, V. Lonnie. (1995, October). What are principals' perceptions of the school library media specialist? *NASSP Bulletin, 79* (573), pp. 72–80.

Eisenberg, Michael B., & Berkowitz, Robert E. (1990). *Information problem-solving: The Big Six Skills Approach to library & information skills instruction.* Norwood, NJ: Ablex Publishing.

Eisenberg, Michael B., & Berkowitz, Robert E. (1992). *Curriculum initiative: An agenda and strategy for library media programs.* Norwood, NJ: Ablex Publishing.

Eisenberg, Michael B., & Johnson, Doug. (1996, March). Computer skills for information problem-solving: Learning and teaching technology in context. (ERIC Digest EDO-IR-96–04.) [Online], 1–8. Available: <http://ericir.syr.edu/ithome/digests/computerskills.html>.

Eisenberg, Michael B., & Milbury, Peter. (1996). LM_NET: Helping school library media specialists to shape the networking revolution in the schools. In Carol Collier Kuhlthau (Ed.), *The virtual school library: Gateway to the information superhighway* (pp. 29–49). Englewood, CO: Libraries Unlimited.

Englert, Richard M. (1982, Spring). Locally based research and the school library media specialist: Guidelines and procedures to use in developing local research projects. *School Library Media Quarterly, 10,* (3), pp. 246–253.

Farmer, Lesley S. J. (1991). *Cooperative learning activities in the library media center.* Englewood, CO: Libraries Unlimited.

Fast Facts. (1998, August 15). Recent statistics from the Library Research Service. *Colorado Department of Education, ED3/110* (141), pp. 1–2.

Fitzpatrick, Kathleen A. (1998). *Program evaluation: Library media services.* Schaumburg, IL: National Study of School Evaluation.

Fullan, Michael G. (1991). *The new meaning of educational change* (2nd ed. with Suzanne Stiegelbauer). New York: Teachers College, Columbia University.

Gardner, Howard. (1983). *Frames of mind: The theory of multiple intelligences.* New York: Basic Books.

Giambra, Carolyn. (1998, January–February). "Libraries Change Lives": Advocacy campaign begins in New York. *Emergency Librarian, 23* (3), pp. 18–19.

Gibson, James L., Ivancevich, John M., & Donnelly, James H. Jr. (1988). *Organizations: Behavior structure processes* (6th ed.). Plano, TX: Business Publications.

Hartzell, Gary N. (1994). *Building influence for the school librarian.* Worthington, OH: Linworth Publishing.

Haycock, Carol-Ann. (1991a). The changing role: From theory to reality. *School Library Media Annual, 9,* pp. 61–67.

Haycock, Carol-Ann. (1991b, November). *Collaboration . . . skills for success.* New York: New York Library Association Conference.

Haycock, Carol-Ann. (1991c, May). Resource-based learning: A shift in the roles of teacher, learner. *NAASP Bulletin, 75* (535), pp. 15–22.

Haycock, Ken. (1990). *Program advocacy: Power, publicity, and the teacher-librarian.* Englewood, CO: Libraries Unlimited.

Haycock, Ken. (1992). *What works: Research about teaching and learning through the school's library resource center.* Seattle, WA: Rockland Press.

Herman, Joan L., Aschbacher, Pamela R., & Winters, Lynn. (1992). *A practical guide to alternative assessment.* Alexandria, VA: Association for Supervision and Curriculum Development.

Herrin, Barbara, Pointon, Louis R., & Russell, Sara. (1986, Spring). Personality and communications behaviors of model school library media specialists. *Drexel Library Quarterly, 21* (2), pp. 69–89.

Howe, Eleanor. (1998, September/October). Make your library media center count. *Knowledge Quest, 27* (1), pp. 28–30.

Hug, William E. (1988, Winter). School library media education and professional development. *School Library Media Quarterly, 16* (2), pp. 115–118.

Ingersoll, Richard M., & Han, Mei. (1994, November). *School library media centers in the United States: 1990–91.* (National Center for Education Statistics 94–326). Washington, DC: U.S. Department of Education.

Isom, Angela. (1991). Collaborative planning: The teacher's and administrator's perspective. Unpublished manuscript, Georgia State University at Atlanta.

Jacobs, Heidi Hayes (Ed.). (1989). *Interdisciplinary curriculum: Design and implementation*. Alexandria, VA: Association for Supervision and Curriculum Development.

Jacobs, Heidi Hayes. (1997, October). *Designing staff development from student assessment data. Curriculum Designs, Inc*. Orlando, FL: ASCD Conference on Teaching & Learning, p. 11.

Johnson, David W., & Johnson, Roger T. (1987). *Learning together and alone: Cooperative, competitive, and individualistic learning* (2nd ed.). Engelwood Cliffs, NJ: Prentice-Hall.

Kanter, Rosabeth Moss. (1987). *Change master I: Understanding the theory*. Encyclopedia Britannica Educational Corp. Video, Color, 29 minutes.

Katims, Michael. (1999, January). *Assessment reform overview*. West Seneca, NY: Erie #1 BOCES Workshop.

Kearney, Carol. (1990). Staff development. In Blanche Woolls (Ed.), *Supervision of district level library media programs* (pp. 52–61). Englewood, CO: Libraries Unlimited.

Kearney, Carol. (1991, Fall). Stuffing or pearls: Flexible scheduling of library media programs. *SAANYS Journal, 22* (2), pp. 19–21.

Kolencik, Patricia L. (1998, May–June). Communicating with administrators: Try a survey. *The Book Report, 17*, pp. 14, 15.

Kouzes, James M., & Posner, Barry Z. (1987). *The leadership challenge: How to get extraordinary things done in organizations*. San Francisco: Jossey-Bass.

Krashen, Stephen. (1993). *The power of reading: Insights from the research*. Englewood, CO: Libraries Unlimited.

Kroll, Carol. (1994). Library media specialists move center stage: An example of implementation of information technologies. *School Library Media Annual, 12*, pp. 70–75.

Kuhlthau, Carol Collier. (1994a). Assessing the library research process. In Carol Collier Kuhlthau (Ed.), *Assessment and the school library media center* (pp. 59–65). Englewood, CO: Libraries Unlimited.

Kuhlthau, Carol Collier. (1994b). *Teaching the library research process* (2nd ed.). Metuchen, NJ: Scarecrow Press.

Kuhlthau, Carol Collier (Ed.). (1996). *The virtual school library: Gateway to the information superhighway*. Englewood, CO: Libraries Unlimited.

Lance, Keith Curry, Welborn, Lynda, & Hamilton-Pennell, Christine. (1992). *The impact of school library media centers on academic achievement*. Washington, DC: U.S. Department of Education.

Learning Pyramid. (n.d.). Bethel, ME: National Training Laboratories.

Loertscher, David V. (1988). *Taxonomies of the school library media program*. Englewood, CO: Libraries Unlimited.

Loertscher, David V. (1996). *Collection mapping in the LMC: Building access in a world of technology*. Castle Rock, CO: Hi Willow Research and Publishing.

Loertscher, David V., & Stroud, Janet G. (1976). *Purdue Self-Evaluation System for media centers*. West Lafayette, IN: Purdue Research Foundation.

Loucks-Horsley, Susan, Harding, Catherine K., Arbuckle, Margaret A., Murray, Lynn B., Dubea, Cynthia, & Williams, Martha K. (1987). *Continuing to learn:*

A guidebook for teacher development. Andover, MA: Regional Laboratory for Educational Improvement of the Northeast and Islands.

Mankato (MN) Grade level benchmarks for media and technology. (n.d.). Mankato, MN. (On-line). 1–15. Available: <http://www.isd77.k12.mm.us/resources/infocurr/benchmark.html>.

Mankato Schools Information literacy curriculum guidelines. (1996). Mankato, MN. (On-line). 1–8. Available: <http://www.isd77.k12.mn.us/resources/infocurr/infolit.html>.

Marris, P. (1975). *Loss and change.* New York: Anchor Press/Doubleday.

Martin, Betty. (1982, Fall). Interpersonal relations and the school library media specialist. *School Library Media Quarterly, 11* (1), pp. 43–44, 53–57.

McGregor, Joy H. (1999, June). *Implementing flexible scheduling in elementary school library centers.* New Orleans: American Library Association Conference.

McKenzie, Michael. (1993). Changing attitudes. In Ben B. Carson and Jane Bandy Smith (Eds.), *Renewal at the schoolhouse: Management ideas for library media specialists and administrators* (pp. 85–93). Englewood, CO: Libraries Unlimited.

Meyer, Jeanette, & Newton, Earle. (1992, November–December). Teachers' views of the implementation of resource-based learning. *Emergency Librarian, 20* (2), pp 13–18.

Milbury, Peter. (1996). Access to computer telecommunications through CORE/Internet at the Pleasant Valley High School: A letter to readers. In Carol Collier Kuhlthau (Ed.), *The virtual school library: Gateway to the information superhighway* (pp. 107–112). Englewood, CO: Libraries Unlimited.

Milbury, Peter. (1998, January–February). Web collection development: Strategies for teacher-librarian collaboration. *Knowledge Quest, 27* (3), pp. 40–41.

Milken Exchange on Education Technology. (1998). Education technology certification standards for educators: State-by-state education technology policy. [On-line]. 1–2. Available: <http://206.117.127.97/statepolicy/compcharts.taf?chart=3>.

Mycio, Geri S. (1992). *Leadership.* Buffalo, NY: Continuous Improvement Strategies.

Mycio, Geri. (1994a). *Communications skills.* Buffalo, NY: Continuous Improvement Strategies.

Mycio, Geri. (1994b). *Listening skills.* Buffalo, NY: Continuous Improvement Strategies.

Neill, D. M. & Medina, N. J. (1989). Standardized testing: Harmful to educational health. *Phi Delta Kappan, 70* (9), pp. 688–697.

Neuman, Delia. (1994). Alternative assessment: Promises and pitfalls. In Carol Collier Kuhlthau (Ed.), *Assessment and the school library media center* (pp. 67–75). Englewood, CO: Libraries Unlimited.

Olson, Renee (Ed.). (1996, January). Principals give short shrift to librarians' curricular role. *School Library Journal, 42* (1), pp. 12–13.

Pappas, Marjorie L., & Tepe, Ann E. (1997). Pathways to knowledge TM. In *Teaching electronic information skills: A resource guide for grades 9–12* (pp. 1–8). McHenry, IL: Follett Software.

Parry, Terence. (1999, June). *Brain compatible learning: Putting the pieces together.* New Orleans: American Library Association Conference, p. 12.

Partners in action: The library resource centre in the school curriculum. (1982). Ontario, Canada: Ministry of Education.

Peters, C. W. (1991). You can't have authentic assessment without authentic content. *Reading Teacher, 44* (8), pp. 590–591.

Pickard, Patricia W. (1994, January). The instructional consultant role of the library media specialist: A progress report. *School Library Media Activities Monthly, 10* (5), pp. 27–29.

Routman, Regie. (1994). *Invitations: Changing as teachers and learners K–12.* Portsmouth, NH: Heinemann.

Schmuck, Richard A., Runkel, Philip J., Arends, Jane H., & Arends, Richard I. (1977). *The Second handbook of organization development in schools.* Palo Alto, CA: Mayfield Publishing.

Schrock, Kathy. (1999). Kathy Schrock's guide for educators. Building rubrics. [On-line]. pp. 1–2. Available: <http://discoveryschool.com/schrockguide/assess.

html> and <http://www.capecod.net/schrockguide/>.

Senge, Peter M. (1990). *The fifth discipline: The art and practice of the learning organization.* New York: Doubleday/Currency.

Smith, Jane Bandy. (1995). *Achieving a curriculum-based library media center program: The middle school model for change.* Chicago: American Library Association.

Sparks, Dennis. (1994, Fall). A paradigm shift in staff development. *Journal of Staff Development, 15* (4), pp. 26–29.

Stripling, Barbara K. (1994a). Assessment of student performance: The fourth step in the instructional design process. In Carol Collier Kuhlthau (Ed.), *Assessment and the school library media center* (pp. 77–97). Englewood, CO: Libraries Unlimited.

Stripling, Barbara K. (1994b). Practicing authentic assessment in the school library. In Carol Collier Kuhlthau (Ed.), *Assessment and the school library media center* (pp. 103–118). Englewood, CO: Libraries Unlimited.

Stripling, Barbara K., & Pitts, Judy M. (1988). *Brainstorms and blueprints: Teaching library research as a thinking process.* Englewood, CO: Libraries Unlimited.

Strong, Rich. (1997, October). Assessment and instructional strategies for extended blocks of time. Silver Strong & Associates. Orlando, FL: ASCD Conference on Teaching and Learning, p. 18.

Summers, Jan. (1996). Using the internet to enhance teaching and learning. In Carol Collier Kuhlthau (Ed.), *The virtual school library: Gateway to the information superhighway* (pp. 21–27). Englewood, CO: Libraries Unlimited.

Tallman, Julie I., & Donham van Deusen, Jean. (1994a, Fall). Collaborative unit planning—Schedule, time, and participants. Part Three: The 1993–94 AASL/Highsmith Research Award Study. *School Library Media Quarterly, 23* (1), pp. 33–37.

Tallman, Julie I., & Donham van Deusen, Jean. (1994b, Fall). External conditions as they relate to curriculum consultation and information skills instruction by school library media specialists. Part Two: The 1993–94 AASL/Highsmith Research Award Study. *School Library Media Quarterly, 23* (1), pp. 27–31.

Turner, Philip M. (1993). *Helping teachers teach* (2nd ed.) Englewood, CO: Libraries Unlimited.

Turner, Philip M. (1996, Summer). What help do teachers want, and what will
    they do to get it? *School Library Media Quarterly, 24* (4), pp. 208–212.

University of the State of New York. (n.d.). *Learning standards for New York State.*
    Albany, NY: State Education Department.

Watkins, J. Foster, & Craft, Anne Hale. (1988, Winter). Library media specialists
    in a staff development role. *School Library Media Quarterly, 16* (2), pp. 110–
    114.

What works: Research about teaching and learning (1986). Washington, DC: U.S.
    Department of Education.

Wiggins, Grant. (1997, October). Assessing to improve performance: Making use
    of feedback. *CLASS.* Orlando, FL: ASCD Conference on Teaching and
    Learning, pp. 2–6.

Wiggins, Grant, & McTighe, Jay. (1998). *Understanding by design.* Alexandria, VA:
    Association for Supervision and Curriculum Development.

Wilson, Patricia Potter, & MacNeil, Angus J. (1998, September). In the dark:
    What's keeping principals from understanding libraries? *School Library
    Journal, 44* (9), pp. 114–116.

Wolcott, Linda Lanchance. (1994, Spring). Understanding how teachers plan:
    Strategies for successful instructional partnerships. *School Library Media
    Quarterly, 22* (3), pp. 161–165.

Wolcott, Linda L., Lawless, Kimberly, & Hobbs, Deborah (1999, June). *Assessing
    pre-service teachers' knowledge of library media programs.* New Orleans: Amer-
    ican Library Association Conference.

Index

About the Author

CAROL A. KEARNEY is a retired elementary, junior high, and senior high school media specialist, former director of the library media program of the Buffalo, NY public schools, and past president of the New York Library Association. She currently divides her time between New York and Florida.